The

Musical Theatre

Cookbook

Other books by these authors:

A Chronological Outline of World Theatre

The Theatre Lover's Cookbook

Illustrated by Mollie Ann Meserve

The
Musical Theatre
Cookbook

Recipes from
Best Loved
Musicals

BY

Mollie Ann Meserve

AND

Walter J. Meserve

FEEDBACK THEATREBOOKS & PROSPERO PRESS

Manufactured in the United States of America.

Feedback Theatrebooks & Prospero Press
305 Madison Avenue Suite 1146
New York, NY 10165

ISBN 0-937657-16-6

Table of Contents

Musical Theatre in America

The fiftieth anniversary of the opening of *Oklahoma!* on Broadway is certainly something to celebrate, but it still marks a recent event in the history of musical theatre in America. Soon after the Revolution, in fact, William Dunlap, the first professional dramatist in the New World, wrote and produced *The Archers; or, Mountaineers in Switzerland*, 1796. Advertised as a comic opera with music by Benjamin Carr, *The Archers* added a love interest and a lot of spectacle to the story of William Tell shooting an apple from his son's head.

A great many of the plays written by Americans before the Civil War made use of music to some extent, lending credence to the idea that a song might be inserted into a play if the actor or actress could sing. The heroine of John Howard Payne's *Clari; or, the Maid of Milan*, 1823, for example, sings his best known song, "Home, Sweet Home," while Capt. Copp from Payne's *Charles the Second*, 1824, is never allowed to finish his ditty about Admiral Trump "and his crew of Tenbreeches, The Dutch Sons of ___." Samuel Woodworth, author of *The Forest Rose*, 1825, described his play as a comedy with musical accompaniment. His Yankee character, Jonathan Ploughboy, bursts into song occasionally as do many of the Yankees in the numerous Yankee vehicle plays of this era, starting with Royall Tyler's Jonathan in *The Contrast*, 1787.

One of the greatest successes in the history of the New York stage was Benjamin Baker's farce called *A Glance at New York*, which opened on February 2, 1848, featuring Mose, the New York Fireman, and numerous songs, such as the "Jolly Young Waterman" sung by a chorus of newsboys, porters and applewomen in the opening scene. Music was also crucial in the popular works of John Brougham, actor and playwright, whose broad burlesques, such as *Po-Ca-Hon-Tas; or, the Gentle Savage*, 1855, earned him the title of the "Aristophanes of the American Stage."

After the War Between the States music became increasingly important to various forms of theatre in America. There were the minstrel shows (first publicly presented at the Bowery Amphitheatre in New York by the Virginia Minstrels on February 6, 1843), the pantomimes (particularly that of George L. Fox in *Humpty Dumpty*, which opened on March 10, 1868, for a spectacular run of 483 performances), the "leg show" burlesques typified by Lydia Thompson and her British Blonds, and the variety theatre of Tony Pastor, the "Father of American Vaudeville," who was determined to promote a "clean vaudeville" for family audiences. More relevant to the development of modern musical theatre, there was the New York opening on September 12, 1866, of Charles M. Barras' *The Black Crook*, frequently called America's first musical comedy, which ran for sixteen months and was revived throughout the century. According to a contemporary critic for the New York *Tribune*, "The scenery is magnificent; the ballet is beautiful; the drama is -- rubbish."

Others tried to capitalize on the success of *The Black Crook*, and none more sensationally than Edward E. Rice with *Evangeline* in 1874, which Rice called "an American opera-bouffe." *The Brook*, "a laughable and musical extravaganza," by Nate Salsbury (to be better known as William F. Cody's business manager for the Buffalo Bill Wild West Shows), performed in 1879 by Salsbury's Troubadours, was the first full-length musical farce to concentrate on topical materials. There was also the comedy team (1871-1884) of Edward Harrigan and Tony Hart, who sang, danced and played the principal roles in Harrigan's extremely popular farces documenting the international tenor of life on New York's Lower East Side.

Charles Hoyt combined music and farce with such appeal in *A Trip to Chinatown*, 1890, that its record of 650 performances lasted well into the twentieth century, as did the popularity of its songs: "Reuben, Reuben, I've Been Thinking," "After the Ball" and "The Bowery."

Although the revue is not, strictly speaking, musical comedy because it lacks a story line, it is part of that mixture from which modern musical theatre developed. With *The Passing Show*, 1894, annual revues appeared in New York and progressed from the Ziegfeld Follies, starting in 1907, until they peaked during the 1920s with the Grand Street Follies, the George White Scandals and the Earl Carroll Vanities. An article on *The Black Crook* in *Theatre Magazine* of 1929 sums it up: "Father's Forbidden Favorite Was The Forerunner Of The Follies And Scandals Of Today."

Operatic entertainment has existed in America since before the Revolution, sometimes seriously, sometimes simply for fun. More opera than drama, *The Temple of Minerva*, 1781, by Francis Hopkinson, America's first poet-composer and a signer of the Declaration of Independence, was performed in Philadelphia for a meeting between General Washington, a great lover of theatre, and the French minister. For the 1793-94 theatre season in New York, Anne Kemble Hatton wrote a politically oriented opera entitled *Tammany; or, the Indian Chief. Americana; or A New Tale of the Genii*, as produced by John Solee in Charleston in 1798, was described as a "musical and allegorical masque." Perhaps to counter the developing popularity of Italian and German opera in America during the second quarter of the nineteenth century, the word "opera" was frivolously interpreted by such lighthearted writers of burlesque as Charles Walcot, who adapted *Der Freischutz* as *Fried Shots*, and John Brougham. At any rate, by the time the first Gilbert and Sullivan collaboration came to America -- *The H.M.S. Pinafore* during the 1878-79 season -- there was a ready audience. Encouraged by the popularity of this latest British artistry, American composers responded. Along with the many well-forgotten comic operas of the period, there are a few noteworthy pieces: Willard Spencer's *The Little Tycoon*, 1886, produced by Augustin Daly, America's foremost theatrical entrepreneur; *Wang*, 1891, book by J. Cheever Goodwin, music by Woolson Morse, and starring DeWolf Hopper, one of the most popular comics of the period; *Robin Hood*, 1891, libretto by Harry B. Smith with music by Reginald de Koven; and *The Belle of New York*, 1897, book and lyrics by Hugh Morton and music by Gustave A. Kerker.

Diversely influenced by all of this activity during the nineteenth century, musical theatre developed with the new century along three distinct and strong lines: the musical revue, an operetta stimulated by the Viennese School and a new style that would become the basis of modern American musical theatre. Of the musical revue or follies, perhaps enough has been said. Although it reached its greatest popularity during the 1920s, it continued -- most notably with *Pins and Needles*, 1937; *Hellzapoppin*, 1938; *This is the Army*, 1942; *Peepshow*, 1950; *Jacques Brel Is Alive and Well and Living in Paris*, 1968; *Eubie!*, 1978 -- and, it seems, will always be with us.

Blending his Irish-English heritage with German training, Victor Herbert created an American equivalent of the best European operettas, such as *Naughty Marietta*, 1910. Distinct from past conditions, his music required singers with trained voices. With Franz Lehár's *Merry Widow*, 1907, a Viennese mood was established and subsequently promoted by the operettas of such composers as Rudolf Friml -- *Rose Marie*, 1924 -- and Sigmund Romberg -- *The Student Prince*, 1924.

By the 1930s this fascination with romantic opera had diminished, to be replaced by an enthusiasm for the kind of musical comedy created early in the century by George M. Cohan, who became a Broadway star in 1904 singing "Yankee Doodle Boy" in *Little Johnny Jones*. Based upon patriotism and local color, his style emphasized speed, pacing, showmanship and lively songs. By 1910, however, that part of Cohan's career was over, and his particular style was not immediately adopted by others. In spite of some fair music by a youthful Irving Berlin and Jerome Kern, musical comedy was scarcely exciting through the first quarter of the century, although both George Gershwin with *La! La! Lucille*, 1919, and Richard Rodgers with *The Poor Little Ritz Girl*, 1920, had appeared on the scene.

Not until 1927, with the production of *Show Boat*, when Jerome Kern and Oscar Hammerstein, II pointed the way to the serious musical plays of the post World War II era, was there another significant landmark in the progress of musical theatre. In general, however, the 1930s are recognized as the period of great songwriters rather than of great musicals. There was Gershwin with *Girl Crazy*, 1930, and Ethel Merman belting out "I Got Rhythm" or *Porgy and Bess*, 1935, and such songs as "Summertime," "I Got Plenty O' Nuttin'" and "Bess, You Is My Woman Now." There was Cole Porter with *Anything Goes*, again with the trumpet-voiced Ethel Merman singing "You're the Top" and "Blow, Gabriel, Blow." With "Johnny One-Note" from *Babes in Arms*, 1937, Richard Rodgers and Lorenz Hart were at their best in song. With *Pal Joey*, 1940, they wrote their best musical together. It, too, has wonderful songs, such as "Bewitched, Bothered and Bewildered," but it was also something of a shocker with its view of a seamy side of life. Not until it was revived in 1952 was the work fully appreciated.

An so -- to *Oklahoma!*, 1943, the Rodgers and Hammerstein masterpiece which put together in a most effective manner all of the characteristics of musical theatre with which writers and musicians had been experimenting for years: story, characters, dance and songs that follow the story line. *Oklahoma!* set the standard. Many of the musicals that have brought audiences to their feet over the past fifty years you will find mentioned in the following pages -- with some interesting tidbits of information for inquiring minds, as well as some opportunities for memorable dining as you celebrate American Musical Theatre.

Bon appétit!

W. J. M.

♫ SHOW BOAT ♫

Book and lyrics by Oscar Hammerstein, II
Music by Jerome Kern
Opened December 27, 1927, at the Ziegfeld Theatre

Shattering existing conventions of musical comedy, *Show Boat* proved that a musical could deal with serious aspects of society. The American musical was forever changed. Undaunted by Edna Ferber's story, which covers more than thirty years in the lives of a family of show boat performers, Hammerstein and Kern had the help of the great Florenz Ziegfeld and an outstanding cast: Charles Winninger as Cap'n Andy, Helen Morgan as Julie, Howard Marsh as Gaylord Ravenal. And Kern's songs still haunt audiences: "Make Believe," "Ol' Man River," "Bill," "Can't Help Lovin' Dat Man," "Life upon the Wicked Stage." A milestone in musical comedy for its serious theme and combination of theatrical effects, *Show Boat* has had several major revivals, the latest in 1993.

When the Cotton Blossom docks with its floating show, Cap'n Andy is immediately hailed by his admirers. (Act II)

> Captain Andy, Captain Andy,
> Here's your lemon cake and homemade candy.
> Quince preserves and apple brandy.
> Mama sends her best regards to you!

Like Mama's regards, this cake is the best!

CAP'N ANDY'S LEMON CAKE

For a party of 10. Preparation time: 1 hour, plus cooling.

1 box white cake mix
3 egg whites
3 tablespoons fresh lemon juice (not bottled juice!)
2 tablespoons canola or safflower oil
Zest of 2 lemons, grated

1

Preheat the oven to 350°.   Grease and flour 2 8"- 8 1/2"
round pans.

In a large mixing bowl, combine all the ingredients except
the lemon zest.   Add 1 1/2 cups of water.   Beat with an
electric mixer on low speed or by hand until the batter is
just moistened.   Beat with the mixer on medium speed
about 2 minutes.   Add the zest and stir to mix well. Pour
the batter evenly into the pans.   Bake for 30-35 minutes, or
until a toothpick inserted into the center of the cake
comes out clean and the cake pulls away from the sides of
the pan.   Cool the cake in the pans on racks for about 5
minutes.   Remove from the pans and cool completely
before frosting with the following:

SHIP'S WHEEL FROSTING

Preparation time: about 10 minutes.

4 ounces Neufchâtel cheese, softened
4 ounces low-fat stick margarine, softened
1 pound confectioners sugar
4-5 drops pure lemon extract
4-5 drops yellow food coloring
Zest of 1-2 lemons, grated
1 or more fresh lemons or limes, sliced into 1/8" rings

In a large bowl, cream the cheese, margarine and sugar.
Add the lemon extract and food coloring and blend, using
an electric mixer if you wish, until the frosting is very
smooth.   Spread evenly on the top of one layer of the cake.
Place the second layer on top of the first.   Frost the sides
first, then the top.   Sprinkle the top only with the grated
zest.   Gently press the lemon or lime rings into the
frosting on the lower half of the sides of the cake, resting
the bottom of each ring on the cake plate, to encircle the
cake with decorative "ship's wheels."   Cut the cake
between the rings. We like this cake served chilled.

For recipes for homemade candy, see pages 32, 33 and 101.

♫

In Act II, the men and women sing:

> Back in old New York where yo' knife an' fork gently
> sink into juicy little chops of tender pork!
> . . . our home just ain't Dahomey at all.

OLD NEW YORK PORK CHOPS

For a party of 6.   Preparation time: about 1 hour and 30
minutes.

1-2 tablespoons canola or safflower oil
6 3/4" pork chops
1/2 teaspoon salt
Freshly ground black pepper
4 large Irish potatoes, thinly sliced
1-2 onions, finely chopped
12 ounces condensed tomato soup

Preheat the oven to 375°.   In a large skillet heat the oil
over medium heat.   Add the chops in a single layer and
brown on both sides.   Season with salt and pepper and set
aside.

In a large baking dish that has been sprayed with non-stick
spray, arrange the potatoes and onions in alternate layers.
Arrange the chops in a single layer on top of the potatoes
and onions. Spread the soup evenly over the chops, cover
the dish with foil and bake for 1 hour on the lower oven
rack. Serve immediately.

♫ OF THEE I SING ♫

Book by George S. Kaufman and Morrie Ryskind
Music by George Gershwin   Lyrics by Ira Gershwin
Opened December 26, 1931, at the Music Box Theatre

In the spring of 1932 the Pulitzer Prize, for the first time in its history, was awarded to a musical play -- "the original American play performed in New York which shall best represent the educational value and power of the stage." That musical play was *Of Thee I Sing.* (Ironically, there was no way to include the name of George Gershwin on the citation: he was only responsible for the music!) This musical spoof of American politics *was* educational, with its two-pronged plot: the new President of the United States is an unqualified nonentity, and the Vice President a pathetic and forgotten man.   President John P. Wintergreen (played by William Gaxton), elected on the party's platform of Love, talks eloquently out of both sides of his mouth but finally comes to his senses in the matter of choosing a wife.   Victor Moore was sensational as Alexander Throttlebottom, the Vice President who tries valiantly and without much success to find out what he is supposed to do. "Love is Sweeping the Country" became a hit song, as did "Of Thee I Sing, Baby," and the show ran for 331 performances.

Those who know *Of Thee I Sing,* often performed during presidential elections, already understand the importance of corn muffins -- to the plot and to the happiness of all. As a bachelor and candidate, Wintergreen is uncertain of his party's scheme for him to win votes by wooing and marrying the winner of a beauty contest. He expresses his doubts to Mary Turner, who assures him that "every girl can cook." "I can cook, and sew, and make lace curtains, and bake the best darned corn muffins you ever ate." That settles the matter for Wintergreen, who is crazy about corn muffins.

Mary: And I'm the only person in the world who can make them without corn.

Wintergreen immediately rejects the contest winner, Diana Devereaux, and professes his love for Mary, while the contest judges proclaim:

We must declare these muffins
The best we ever ate!

Later, when the jilted Diana threatens to sue, the Supreme Court is forced to decide which is more important: corn muffins or justice!

Chief Justice: The decision of the Supreme Court is --
Corn Muffins!

You may not get to be President, or even First Lady, but you 'll win the popular vote with these muffins:

THE BEST DARNED CORN MUFFINS YOU EVER ATE

Makes 12 muffins.   Preparation time: about 30 minutes.

1/2 cup yellow corn meal
1 cup unbleached flour
1/2 cup whole wheat flour
1/4 cup sugar
1/4 teaspoon salt
2 teaspoons baking powder
1 1/4 cups milk
1 tablespoon canola or safflower oil
2 egg whites

Preheat the oven to 400°. Generously grease a 12-cup muffin tin.

In a large bowl, combine the corn meal, flour, sugar, salt and baking powder. Blend thoroughly. Mix in the milk, oil and egg whites. Fill each muffin cup 3/4 full. Bake for 12 minutes, or until the muffins are lightly browned and pull away from the sides of the cups. Cool briefly before removing from the tin. Serve warm with butter or margarine.

PUT LOVE IN THE WHITE HOUSE

In Act I, Scene 2, the committee discusses the party's ticket. A Southern member speaks:

> Lyons: Gentlemen, you ask me about the South. It is the land of romance, of roses and honeysuckle, of Southern chivalry and hospitality, fried chicken and waffles, salad and coffee.

SOUTHERN HOSPITALITY FRIED CHICKEN

For a party of 4-6. Preparation time: about 1 hour.

3 tablespoons flour
1/4 teaspoon black pepper
1/4 teaspoon white pepper
1/4 teaspoon salt
1/2 teaspoon dried marjoram or oregano
1/2 teaspoon dried rosemary
1 large fryer, cut into serving pieces
1/2 cup (or more) canola or safflower oil

In a paper or plastic bag, shake together the flour, pepper, salt, marjoram or oregano and rosemary. Add the chicken and shake until all pieces are evenly coated. Set aside. Heat a large skillet over medium-high heat. Add enough oil to half cover the chicken. When the oil is hot, add the chicken in a single layer. Reduce the heat to medium, cover and cook for about 15 minutes. Turn the chicken over, cover and cook for 10 minutes. Uncover and cook for 5 minutes.

Remove the chicken from the skillet and drain on several folds of paper toweling. Serve hot, with gravy (see page 155).

SOUTHERN HOSPITALITY WAFFLES

For a party of 4-6. Preparation time: about 20 minutes.

2 cups sifted unbleached flour
1/4 teaspoon salt
3 teaspoons baking powder
2 eggs, separated, or 2 ounces egg substitute and
    2 egg whites
2 cups milk
4 tablespoons melted unsalted butter or margarine

Preheat the waffle iron. Sift together the flour, salt and baking powder. In a large bowl, beat the egg whites until stiff but not dry. In another large bowl, beat the egg yolks and add the milk, mixing thoroughly. Add the dry ingredients and beat by hand until smooth. Stir in the melted butter. Gently fold in the egg whites. Place about 4 tablespoons of the batter into the waffle iron and bake for about 2 minutes or according to your iron's directions. (As waffle irons are unpredictable and varied, you may want to use the first waffle as a test, adjusting the timing according to the results.) Serve the waffles hot with unsalted butter or margarine and your favorite syrup. (Lyons and his cronies might mix their syrup with bacon or sausage drippings, but we *do not* recommend consumption of this fatty concoction!)

♫ BABES IN ARMS ♫

Book, music and lyrics by Richard Rodgers
and Lorenz Hart
Opened April 4, 1937, at the Shubert Theatre

A classic Depression-era show-biz dream: to avoid being sent to a work farm because their parents, old vaudevillians, are working in the Federal Theatre Project at low salaries, a group of kids struggles to put on a musical revue. With a cast including Mitzi Green and Ray Heatherton, with Alfred Drake and Dan Dailey in minor roles, *Babes in Arms* produced a remarkable number of hit songs, more than any other Rodgers and Hart score: "Where or When," "I Wish I Were in Love Again," "My Funny Valentine" and "Johnny One-Note." Costing a mere $55,000 to produce, the show's run of 289 performances made it a great success.

One of the most enduring songs from *Babes in Arms* is "The Lady Is a Tramp." The following lines appealed to us:

> I've wined and dined on Mulligan stew
> And never wished for turkey,
> As I hitched and hiked and drifted, too,
> From Maine to Albuquerque.

MULLIGAN STEW

For a party of 10-12. Preparation time: about 4 hours.

3/4 pound lean stew beef, veal or lamb, cut in 3/4" chunks
3/4 pound pork shoulder, cut in 3/4" chunks
3 1/2 quarts beef or chicken stock
1 3 1/2-pound fryer, cut up
3 ripe tomatoes, peeled, seeded and coarsely chopped

1 cup fresh lima beans
1/2 teaspoon crushed red pepper flakes
2 green bell peppers, membranes and seeds removed,
    chopped
1 large onion, chopped
2 large carrots, scraped and sliced into 1/4" rounds
1 stalk celery, chopped
1 large potato, cut into 3/4" chunks
5-6 pods fresh okra, sliced into 1/2" rounds
1 bay leaf
1 tablespoon Worcestershire sauce
Kernels from 2 ears fresh corn
Salt and freshly ground black pepper, to taste

Place the meat and stock in a large pot and bring to a boil over medium heat. Reduce the heat to simmer and cook for 1 1/2 hours. Add the chicken and return to a boil. Reduce the heat to simmer and cook for 1 hour, or until the chicken falls from the bones. Let the stew stand until the chicken is cool enough to handle. Remove the bones. Return the chicken to the pot and add the tomatoes, lima beans, red pepper flakes, bell peppers, onion, carrots, celery, potato, okra, bay leaf and Worcestershire sauce. Simmer, stirring frequently, for about 45 minutes. Add the corn and simmer for 15 minutes. Season with salt and pepper and serve hot with fresh cornbread or corn muffins (see page 5).

For a recipe for turkey, see page 133.

9

♫ LEAVE IT TO ME ♫

Book by Bella and Samuel Spewack
Music and lyrics by Cole Porter
Opened November 9, 1938, at the Imperial Theatre

This light-hearted spoof of communism and American diplomacy abroad -- based on the Spewacks' comedy, *Clear All Wives* -- was their first venture into the musical genre. It also reunited the great comedy acting team from *Of Thee I Sing*, William Gaxton and the incomparable Victor Moore, who in *Leave It to Me* played Alonzo Goodhue, a bumbler from Topeka, Kansas, appointed ambassador to Russia. The role of Mrs. Goodhue catapulted Sophie Tucker from night club singer to Broadway star. Gene Kelly made his debut as a secretary, and Mary Martin, with "My Heart Belongs to Daddy," became an instant celebrity. A madcap musical, opulently produced, *Leave It to Me* ran for 307 performances.

A man whose heart is always in Topeka, Goodhue sings of his desires in Act II, Scene 2: "I Want to Go Home."

How I long, at the drugstore, again I sit
And order a double banana split,
And then wash it down with some rare old
sars'parilly.
The trouble is with this job
You can't get corn-on-the-cob.

DOUBLE BANANA SPLIT

For a party of 6. Preparation time: about 25 minutes.

1/2 pint whipping cream
Chocolate syrup or fudge topping
1 cup drained canned crushed pineapple

1 cup chopped fresh strawberries
1 cup chopped peanuts
6 bananas
1 pint French vanilla ice cream
1 pint chocolate ice cream
1 pint strawberry ice cream
6 whole maraschino cherries

Chill six serving bowls. A few minutes before serving, whip the cream and heat the chocolate syrup or fudge topping. Divide the pineapple, the strawberries and the peanuts separately into 6 equal portions. Peel the bananas and split each in half, lengthwise. Into each bowl, place both halves of 1 banana, spread apart. Between the banana halves, place a large spoonful each of French vanilla, chocolate and strawberry ice cream. Work rapidly or the ice cream will begin to melt. Sprinkle the ice cream with the crushed pineapple, strawberries and peanuts. Drizzle the warm topping liberally over all the ingredients. Top the splits with the whipped cream and garnish with the cherries. Serve immediately.

TOPEKA, KANSAS, CORN-ON-THE-COB

Preparation time: about 10 minutes.

At least as many ears of fresh corn as there are members
    in your party
Unsalted butter or margarine
Salt

Remove the husks and silk from the corn. Bring enough water to cover the corn to a boil in a very large pot. Drop the ears, one at a time, into the boiling water. Boil rapidly until tender, about 10 minutes. Drain and serve immediately with butter and salt.

KNICKERBOCKER HOLIDAY

♫

Book and lyrics by Maxwell Anderson
Music by Kurt Weill
Opened November 19, 1938,
at the Ethel Barrymore Theatre

Both Anderson and Weill were deeply concerned with the problems facing the world in 1938, and they wanted to say something meaningful about the forces of tyranny and freedom. For his satirical approach to the difficulites he saw, Anderson found inspiration in Washington Irving's *Knickerbocker History of New York* and, particularly, the character of Governor Pieter Stuyvesant, whose despotism Anderson intended as a comment on the activities of President Franklin D. Roosevelt. To promote their cause and their definition of an American as one who should love freedom and abhor restrictions of any kind, the authors created as their hero a tinker whose only serious character deficiency is his complete inability to take orders. Their choice of Walter Huston to play Stuyvesant was a challenge. Huston was a vaudeville song-and-dance man with a limited voice and no experience in Broadway musicals, but Anderson and Weill solved all problems with the most memorable song in the show: "September Song."

To express their convictions about world conditions, Anderson and Weill drew modern and melodramatic parallels with the various suppressions that Stuyvesant forced upon the population of New Amsterdam. One of these parallels appears in the "Ballad of the Robbers."

> When first men fled from Eden fair . . .
> The honest men were much amazed
> By thieves that hung around.
> They stole the horses from the barns,
> They stole the eggs and hams.

(Then men made laws, and now . . .)
The honest men sit in the jails,
The robbers they are out.

While not acknowledging that any thief would know a timbale from a turnip, we offer our suggestion for serving up some of their ill-gotten gains in a pleasing manner.

HAM TIMBALES WITH EGG GRAVY

For a party of 6.   Preparation time: about 45 minutes.

3 cups ground cooked ham
1/2 cup soft bread crumbs
Paprika, to taste
4 eggs, well beaten
1 1/2 cups scalded milk

For the gravy:
2 cups milk
4 tablespoons unsalted butter or margarine, softened
4 tablespoons flour
2 hard-boiled eggs, coarsely chopped
Salt and freshly ground black pepper, to taste

Preheat the oven to 350°. In a large bowl, combine the ham, bread crumbs and paprika. Stir in the eggs and milk. Divide the mixture into 12 equal portions and place in well greased muffin cups. Bake for 30 minutes.

While the timbales bake, make the gravy: Place the milk in the top of a double boiler and heat over boiling water. Combine the butter and flour to make a roux, drop into the hot milk, remove from the heat and let stand for 15 minutes. Beat until smooth, stir in the eggs, salt and pepper and serve over the hot timbales.

♫ PAL JOEY ♫

Book by John O'Hara   Music by Richard Rodgers
Lyrics by Lorenz Hart
Opened December 25, 1940, at the Ethel Barrymore Theatre

"Although it is expertly done, can you draw sweet water from a foul well?" With this question, critic Brooks Atkinson gave voice to the doubts that many audience members felt after seeing *Pal Joey*. Following the adventures of Joey Evans -- played by Gene Kelly -- a heel, congenial liar and unscrupulous womanizer who dances his way into too many hearts, *Pal Joey* broke many of the popular sentimental rules of musical comedy. Not until 1952, when it was revived by Jule Styne and Leonard Key, was it fully appreciated for its realistic characters and dialogue, as well as for songs such as "Bewitched, Bothered and Bewildered" and "The Flower Garden of My Heart."

In the second act, Ludlow Lowell, an "agent," pressures Joey to audition for the Staff O'Life Bread program. He ballyhoos Staffo bread and the various Staffo trucks with their sides painted to advertise bread, pies, cakes, cinnamon buns and ginger snaps. Actually, Lowell is scheming to blackmail the owner of Staffo, whose wife has helped Joey. Whatever Lowell's low intentions, however, the bread is delicious.

STAFFO DESSERT BREAD

For a party of 8-10. Preparation time: about 1 hour and 30 minutes.

1 1/2 cups sugar
8 ounces unsalted butter or margarine, softened
1 teaspoon pure vanilla extract

14

2 eggs or 4 ounces egg substitute
2 1/2 cups unbleached flour
1 cup sour cream or non-fat sour cream
1 1/2 teaspoons baking soda
2-3 teaspoons cinnamon
1/2 cup chopped pecans or walnuts

Preheat the oven to 325°. In a large bowl, cream 1 cup of the sugar, the butter and the vanilla extract. Add the eggs and beat well. Mix in the flour, sour cream and baking soda and beat well. In a small bowl, mix the remaining sugar with the cinnamon and nuts. Place 1/2 of the batter in a well greased 9" tube pan and top with 3/4 of the cinnamon mixture. Without stirring, add the remaining batter to the pan. Carefully swirl the remaining cinnamon mixture through the batter. Bake for about 1 hour. Allow to cool for a few minutes before cutting. Serve warm.

STAFFO APPLE TURNOVERS

For a party of 12.   Preparation time: about 45 minutes.

For the filling:
1 tablespoon margarine
2 large or 3 small golden delicious apples, peeled, cored
    and diced
1 tablespoon vinegar
1 tablespoon fresh lemon juice
Zest of 1 lemon, grated
3/4 cup sugar
1 teaspoon cinnamon
1/4 teaspoon nutmeg

For the crust:
1 teaspoon vinegar
1/2 cup milk
1 cup vegetable shortening
2 cups unbleached flour
Sugar, for topping

In a large skillet, melt the margarine over medium-high heat. Add the apples, vinegar, lemon juice, zest, sugar, cinnamon and nutmeg and cook, stirring frequently, until the apples are tender.

While the apples cook, make the crust: Preheat the oven to 350°. In a small bowl, stir the vinegar into the milk. Set aside. In a large bowl, cut the shortening into the flour, add the milk and work into a dough (the dough will be very sticky). Divide the dough into 2 equal portions. On a well floured surface, roll out each portion into a rectangle 1/8" thick. Cut each rectangle into half a dozen 6" squares. Arrange the squares, not touching, along the sides of well greased baking sheets, with half of each square overlapping the edge of the sheet. Place about 2 tablespoons of the apple mixture near the center of each square. Fold the outer half of each square over the half resting on the sheet, aligning the edges. Seal the edges with a fork. Pierce the tops of the turnovers several times with the fork and sprinkle with sugar. Bake for about 18-20 minutes. Allow to cool before dividing each turnover in half. Serve as finger food or on individual plates, topped with vanilla ice cream.

♫ LADY IN THE DARK ♫

Book by Moss Hart   Music by Kurt Weill
Lyrics by Ira Gershwin
Opened January 23, 1941, at the Alvin Theatre

The "Lady in the Dark," played by Gertrude Lawrence, is Liza Elliott, a magazine editor who attempts to resolve the romantic and professional complications of her life through psychoanalysis. Because Moss Hart had just undergone psychoanalysis, he was eager to write a somewhat serious work, and although the music is dramatically basic to the structure of the play, it is, except for the first scene, confined to the dream sequences.

Both Victor Mature and Macdonald Carey had roles in *Lady in the Dark,* but it was Danny Kaye who nearly stole the show with his tongue-twisting rendition of "Tschaikowsky." As the Ringmaster who introduces "The Greatest Show on Earth, Liza Elliot's Gargantuan Three-Ring Circus" in one of the dream sequences, Kaye, true to his specialty, rattled off the names of forty-nine Russian composers in thirty-nine seconds.

In Act I, Scene 2, Maggie tells Liza about her experiences with an analyst:

> But it would be awfully hard to make me believe that the reason I can't stand artichokes is because my mother put me on the pottie wrong when I was two years old.

Without comment, but with one basic assumption, we offer our recipe for artichokes.

ARTICHOKES AU GRATIN

For a party of 6.   Preparation time: about 40 minutes.

2 14-ounce cans artichoke hearts, well drained
1/4 cup unsalted butter or margarine
1 clove garlic, minced
1/2 teaspoon freshly grated black pepper
1/3 cup flour, sifted
1 1/2 cups milk
1 egg, slightly beaten
1/2 cup grated Swiss cheese
1 tablespoon finely crushed dry bread crumbs
1 teaspoon paprika

Preheat the oven to 450°.   Cut the artichoke hearts into very thin slices. In a large skillet, melt the butter over medium heat, add the artichokes and garlic and sauté for 5-7 minutes. With a slotted spoon, remove the artichokes from the skillet and arrange in a single layer in a baking dish that has been sprayed with non-stick spray. Stir the pepper and flour into the butter remaining in the skillet. Add the milk, a bit at a time, stirring constantly. Reduce the heat to simmer and cook, still stirring constantly, until thickened. Remove from the heat and set aside. Combine the egg and 1/4 cup of the cheese in a large bowl and stir in the liquid from the skillet. Blend until smooth. Pour the mixture over the artichokes, sprinkle evenly with the remaining cheese, bread crumbs and paprika. Bake for about 15 minutes, or until golden. Serve immediately.

♫ OKLAHOMA! ♫

Book, music and lyrics by Richard Rodgers
and Oscar Hammerstein, II
Opened April 1, 1943, at the St. James Theatre

"Jubilant and enchanting!" was the decision in 1943. Since then critics, scholars and audiences have praised this thoroughly American show, with its artful and imaginative synthesis of song, story and dance, as a milepost in the development of musical theatre. Certainly, *Oklahoma!* was a wonderful beginning for Broadway's most famous team, and it gave major roles to Alfred Drake as Curly, Joan Roberts as Laury and Celeste Holm as Ado Annie. A liberal adaptation of Lynn Rigg's play, *Green Grow the Lilacs*, set in the Oklahoma Territory in 1907, *Oklahoma!* provided a necessary entertainment for a country thoroughly engaged in World War II. Its record run of five years and nine weeks was not broken until 1961, by *My Fair Lady*.

Ado Annie explains in the second act that "Kissin's my favorite food." Assuming that everyone already has that recipe, we will move on to other delicacies. The first reference to food is found in Curly's joyful song, "Oh, What a Beautiful Morning."

> The corn is as high as an elephant's eye
> An' it looks like it's climbin' clear up to the sky.

If you would like recipes for corn, they appear on pages 11 and 151.

A little later in the first scene, Gertie looks into Laury's lunch hamper:

> Gertie: You got gooseberry tarts, too. Wonder if they is as light as mine. Mine'd like to float away if you blew on them.

Laury: I did blow on one of mine and it broke up into a million pieces.

So will ours!

GOOSEBERRY TARTS

Makes 18 2" tarts.   Preparation time: about 1 hour, plus chilling.

For the tart shells:
2 cups unbleached flour
6 ounces Neufchâtel cheese, softened
2 sticks margarine, softened

For the filling:
5 cups fresh gooseberries, washed and picked over
1 1/4 cups (or more) sugar
1/3 cup flour
1 teaspoon cinnamon
1 tablespoon quick-cooking tapioca

Preheat the oven to 450°.   Sift the flour into a large bowl. Cut in the cheese and margarine and blend well to make a dough. On a well floured surface, roll out the dough to a thickness of 1/8". Form the dough over the well greased bottoms of 18 2" muffin cups and bake for 12 minutes. Allow to cool before filling.

While the shells cool, prepare the filling: Place the gooseberries in a large bowl. Combine the sugar, flour, cinnamon and tapioca and gently stir this mixture into the gooseberries until thoroughly blended. Let stand for a few minutes.

Reduce the oven heat to 350°. Spoon equal portions of filling into each tart shell. Place the tarts on a baking sheet and bake until the top edges of the crust brown, about 20 minutes. Serve warm or at room temperature.

In Act II, Scene 1, at the picnic, Nick shouts: "Hey, Ado Annie, y' got that same sweet-pertater pie like last year?" "You bet," answers Ado Annie, and we have her recipe.

ADO ANNIE'S SWEET-PERTATER PIE

For a party of 6-8. Preparation time: about 1 hour and 20 minutes, including baking.

For the crust:
1/4 cup milk
1/2 teaspoon vinegar
1 cup unbleached flour
1/2 cup vegetable shortening

For the filling:
2 large sweet potatoes, peeled and cut into 2" chunks
1/4 cup light brown sugar
1/4 cup granulated sugar
1/8 teaspoon salt
1 teaspoon cinnamon
A grating of fresh nutmeg
1/4 cup half-and-half
12 marshmallows, split in half, crosswise

Preheat the oven to 400°. In a small bowl or cup, combine the milk and vinegar. In a large bowl, cream the flour and shortening. Add the milk and work with a fork until completely blended. The dough will be moist; so dust your hands liberally with flour as you form the dough into a ball. Place the ball on a well floured surface and, with a well floured rolling pin, roll into a circle just large enough to fit your pie pan. Once the crust is in the pan, line it with foil and fill with pewter pellets. Brown the crust for 12 minutes. Remove the pellets and foil and allow the crust to cool before filling. Reduce the oven heat to 350°.

Meanwhile, boil the potatoes in a large pot until very tender. Drain the potatoes and place them in a large bowl.

21

Add the sugar, salt, cinnamon, nutmeg and half-and-half. Mash and mix until the mixture is smooth and the ingredients are thoroughly blended. With an electric mixer on medium speed, beat until light and fluffy. Spoon the mixture into the crust and bake for 20 minutes. Top with the marshmallows and continue baking for 10-15 minutes, or until the marshmallows are melting and golden. Serve the pie warm or at room temperature.

♬

Later in the scene, Aunt Eller is a little worried as she coaxes Carnes to choose the right partner for lunch: "Not fer cold duck with stuffin' and that lemon-meringue pie?" Well . . . maybe. Try the pie, anyway.

OKLAHOMA STYLE LEMON-MERINGUE PIE

For a party of 6-8. Preparation time: about 1 hour, plus cooling.

For the crust:
1/2 teaspoon vinegar
1/3 cup milk
1/3 cup vegetable shortening
1 1/3 cups unbleached flour

For the filling:
1/4 cup unbleached flour
1 1/4 cups sugar
3 tablespoons cornstarch
1/8 teaspoon (or less) salt
3 egg yolks
1 tablespoon unsalted butter or margarine
Juice of 2-3 lemons
Zest of 2-3 lemons, grated

For the meringue:
3 egg whites
1/4 teaspoon cream of tartar
6 tablespoons sugar

Preheat the oven to 450°. Stir the vinegar into the milk and set aside. Cut the shortening into the flour and blend thoroughly. Add the milk and, with well floured hands, work into a very sticky dough. On a well floured surface, roll out the dough into a circle 1/8" thick. Line a 9" pie pan with the dough. Place a sheet of aluminum foil gently over the crust, covering the edge. Gently spread pewter pellets evenly on the bottom of the foil-lined crust and bake for 12 minutes. Remove the pellets and foil and allow the crust to cool before filling.

Reduce the oven heat to 325°. While the crust cools, make the filling. In a large saucepan, combine the flour, sugar, cornstarch and salt. Stir in 3 cups of cold water. Place the pan over low heat and cook, stirring constantly, until the mixture is thick and clear, about 15 minutes. Place the egg yolks in a small bowl, add about 1/4 cup of the hot flour mixture and stir until thoroughly blended. Add the egg yolk mixture to the saucepan and stir until blended. Stir in the butter, lemon juice and zest. Remove the filling from the heat and allow to cool for a few minutes before pouring into the crust.

Place the egg whites in a large bowl and beat until frothy. Gradually beat in the cream of tartar and sugar and continue beating until stiff peaks form. Cover the filling with the meringue (do not cover the edge of the crust!). Bake for about 15 minutes, or until the meringue is golden. Cool on a rack for a few minutes before cutting, or serve chilled.

♫ CARMEN JONES ♫

Adapted by Oscar Hammerstein, II
Opened December 2, 1943, at the Broadway Theatre

Hammerstein set out to write a modern version of the opera *Carmen*, using Prosper Merimée's words, George's Bizet's music and an all-black cast. "The nearest thing," he argued, "in our modern American life to an equivalent of the gypsies in Spain is the Negro." Changing the setting to a Southern parachute factory during World War II, he created a vividly theatrical piece that was successfully revived at London's Old Vic Theatre in 1991. In the original production, Muriel Smith and Muriel Rahn played Carmen; Luther Saxon and Napoleon Reed played Joe.

In Act I, Scene 3, at Billy Pastor's Café, Joe gives Carmen a box of "Marshmeller fudge."

JOE'S MARSHMELLER FUDGE

For a party of 10-12. Preparation time: about 20 minutes, plus cooling.

4 cups sugar
14 ounces evaporated milk
1/4 cup unsalted butter or margarine
1 pint marshmallow creme
1/2 cup chopped walnuts
6 ounces chocolate chips
1 teaspoon pure vanilla extract

In a large saucepan, bring the sugar, milk and butter to a boil. Cook rapidly for 11 minutes, stirring occasionally. Stir in the marshmallow creme, nuts, chocolate chips and vanilla extract and stir until the marshmallow creme and chips are melted. Pour into a buttered 9" x 12" pan. Allow to cool completely before cutting.

In Act II, Scene 2, at the baseball park the night of the big fight, there is a lot of singing:

Men: Go fish fer fish
       Dat you can fry!

FRIED FISH

For a party of 6.   Preparation time: about 25 minutes.

Vegetable oil, for deep frying
1/8 teaspoon salt
1/2 cup flour
3 pounds haddock, catfish or trout fillets
1 egg or 2 ounces egg substitute
4 tablespoons milk
2 cups fine dry bread crumbs

Preheat the oil in the deep fryer.   Combine the salt and flour and dredge the fillets in the mixture.   In a flat-bottomed bowl, beat together the egg and milk. Dip the fillets into the mixture, coating well. Dredge the fillets evenly in the bread crumbs. Deep fry for about 15 minutes or until golden brown. Serve immediately.

♫ CAROUSEL ♫

Book, music and lyrics by Richard Rodgers
and Oscar Hammerstein, II
Opened April 19, 1945, at the Majestic Theatre

Ferenc Molnar's *Liliom* (1921) at first seemed too tragic as the basis of a musical, but Rodgers and Hammerstein made just the right changes. They shifted the scene from Budapest to the coast of Maine, added choruses of Yankee workers, and in the final song provided that essential emotion that everyone needs: "With hope in your heart/ You'll never walk alone." John Raitt as the irresponsible carnival barker and Jan Clayton as the girl who falls innocently in love with him celebrated the joy of living in "June is Bustin' Out All Over" and admitted their uncertainty in "If I Loved You." *Carousel* was a great success and for about two years played directly across West 44th Street from *Oklahoma!*

In Act II, Scene 1, a clambake on an island provides "codfish chowder with onions floating on top," red-hot lobsters "doused in melted butter," and clams "steamed under rockweed/And poppin' from their shells."

POOR MAN'S MAINE CHOWDER

For a party of 6-8. Preparation time: about 30 minutes.

3-4 new potatoes in their jackets, diced
1 stalk celery, chopped
1 large carrot, scraped and chopped
2 tablespoons unsalted butter or margarine
1 large onion, finely chopped
1 tablespoon flour
1 28-ounce can crushed tomatoes in their liquid
3 cups cod cheeks and tongues (if salted, soaked overnight in cold water)
Salt and freshly ground black or white pepper, to taste

In a large saucepan, bring 3 cups of water to a boil. Add the potatoes, celery and carrot and cook until tender, about 15 minutes. Drain the vegetables, reserving the cooking water.

While the vegetables cook, melt the butter in a large skillet over medium heat. Add the onion and sauté until translucent. Stir in the flour and cook until it begins to brown. Add the tomatoes and the reserved cooking water. Bring to a boil, stirring constantly, until the mixture begins to thicken. Reduce the heat to simmer, add the cheeks and tongues and cook gently for about 5 minutes, adding more water if the chowder becomes too thick. Add the potatoes, celery and carrot and simmer until heated through. Add salt and pepper and serve hot.

A SEASIDE CLAMBAKE

For a party of 12. Preparation time: about 4 hours.

1 dozen ears sweet corn
1 dozen soft shell or 5 dozen hard shell clams, scrubbed
3 fryers, quartered
8 sweet or Irish potatoes
1 dozen 1 1/2-pound hard shell lobsters
Several sticks unsalted butter, clarified

You will need a sturdy shovel or two, a large number of smooth round rocks, a wet tarpaulin about 4' square, hardwood for your fire (with a little driftwood -- in keeping with the spirit of the musical), about 3 1/2 bushels of seaweed, cheesecloth, a rake, a bucket of sea water and plenty of wet hand cloths. And don't forget fire-proof tongs and a box of matches!

Dig a sand pit about 3' square and 1' deep. Line the pit with rocks (not shale!). Using the hardwood, build a fire over the rocks. Keep feeding the fire while the rocks heat, about 3 hours. Meanwhile, collect the seaweed and wash it in fresh water. Keep the seaweed soaking until ready to use.

Partially husk the corn, leaving the last two layers of husks intact. Pull these layers back far enough to remove the silk, then replace them to cover the kernels. Reserve the removed husks. Divide the food into 12 equal portions and wrap each in cheesecloth. When the rocks are hot, rake the embers from the pit. Line the rock pit with the seaweed to a depth of about 6". Place the packets of food in a single layer in the pit, cover with the corn husks and sprinkle with sea water. Quickly cover the pit with the wet tarp, weighing it down securely with rocks. Allow the food to steam, undisturbed, for about 1 hour. When the tarp "puffs up," check for doneness by lifting the tarp at one corner (carefully!). If the clams have opened, the food is done.

A few minutes before opening the pit, clarify the butter: Melt the butter over low heat and allow to stand until the milk solids have settled to the bottom. Skim the clear yellow butter fat from the top and strain into small serving bowls. Use the clarified butter for dipping the clams and lobster meat.

ANNIE GET YOUR GUN

Book by Dorothy and Herbert Fields
Music and lyrics by Irving Berlin
Opened May 16, 1946, at the Imperial Theatre

If the American theatre has an unofficial anthem, it is "There's No Business Like Show Business." And this is just one of the nine Irving Berlin songs that Ethel Merman trumpeted from the stage of the Imperial Theatre, songs like "Doin' What Comes Natur'lly," "They Say It's Wonderful," "You Can't Get a Man with a Gun," and "I Got the Sun in the Morning." Wolcott Gibbs declared that her "voice might easily have tumbled the walls of Jerico."

Annie Get Your Gun ran for 1,147 performances. Twenty years later, in 1966, Ethel Merman repeated her role as Annie in a major revival at Lincoln Center.

As Annie Oakley first walks onto the stage in Act I, "two birds are dangling over her shoulder." Having shot her birds through the head, as she always does, she wants to sell them to the hotel proprietor. "Birds make mighty fine eating," she says. And she's right!

ANNIE OAKLEY'S BAKED GAME BIRDS

For a party of 6. Preparation time: about 4 hours and 30 minutes, after overnight soaking.

For the game:
2 pheasants or partridges, skinned and cleaned
1 pound salt pork, thinly sliced

For the dressing:
1 loaf white bread, broken into large pieces
4 medium onions, coarsely chopped
1 teaspoon poultry seasoning
Salt and freshly ground black pepper, to taste

29

In a large pot, cover the birds with salted water and soak overnight.

Preheat the oven to 275°. In a large bowl, using your hands, combine the bread, onions, poultry seasoning and salt and pepper. Mix well but do not compress.

Drain the birds and blot dry with paper towels. Place the birds, breast side up, on a well greased rack in a roasting pan. Cover each bird with strips of salt pork and a generous coating of the dressing. Pour enough water into the pan to reach a depth of 1". Cover the pan with a tightly fitting lid or heavy-duty foil. Bake for 4 hours, adding more water as necessary to maintain 1" in the pan. Remove the birds from the oven and allow to stand for 10 minutes before carving.

♫

In Act II, Scene 2, Annie is a hungry guest, along with Pawnee Bill and Buffalo Bill, at the Long Island home of Mrs. Schuyler Adams. Unfortunately, each time a waiter gives Annie a plate of salad, interruptions intrude and the salad is ushered out before she can eat it.

ANNIE'S VANISHING SALAD

For a party of 6. Preparation time: about 20 minutes.

2 ripe tomatoes, cut into thin wedges
2 cups cooked, chilled penne or other pasta
4 tablespoons mild salsa
1 cup sliced fresh mushrooms
1/4 cup thinly sliced red bell pepper
1/4 cup thinly sliced green bell pepper
1/4 cup coarsely chopped pitted ripe olives
1 teaspoon ground cumin

1 tablespoon whole fennel seeds
Freshly ground black pepper, to taste
1/4 cup shredded cheddar cheese
2 ripe avocados, peeled, pitted and cut into 1/2" chunks
6 large leaves green leaf or red leaf lettuce

In a large bowl toss together all the ingredients except the avocados and lettuce. Very gently toss in the avocados. Arrange the lettuce leaves in a large bowl or on individual plates and top with the salad.

♫ BRIGADOON ♫

Book and lyrics by Alan Jay Lerner
Music by Frederick Loewe
Opened on March 13, 1947, at the Ziegfeld Theatre

Often revived, this story of a magical Scottish village that comes to life only once every hundred years is distinguished for a blending of theatrical effects that is successful in capturing the essence of Scottish fancy. Agnes de Mille's dances (the Sword Dance, the Chase, the Funeral Dance) had never been better realized as part of an unfolding story. The songs -- "Brigadoon," "The Heather on the Hill," "Almost Like Being in Love" -- still charm audiences, as they did those who, in post-War America, kept *Brigadoon* running for 581 performances.

The time is "May of this year." An early scene takes place in the village square -- MacConnachy Square -- where Sandy has a booth at the fair and encourages customers.

> Come over to Sandy's booth
> I'm sellin' the sweetest candy here
>   That ever shook loose a tooth.
> I eat it myself an' there's no doubt
> 'Tis creamy an' good an' thick --
> So, laddies, I hope ye'll buy me out,
> 'Tis makin' me kind o' sick.

We suggest moderation, however difficult to achieve.

SANDY'S CANDY

Makes about 2 pounds of candy. Preparation time: about 30 minutes, plus standing.

3 cups sugar
3/4 cup light corn syrup
3 egg whites
1 3-ounce package sugar-free cherry jello

3/4 cup chopped nuts
1 teaspoon pure vanilla extract

In a saucepan, mix the sugar, corn syrup and 3/4 cup of water. Cook until your candy thermometer reads 260°. Meanwhile, beat the egg whites until soft peaks form. Add the jello and beat until the mixture is soft and glossy. Very slowly (as in trickle) and beating constantly, pour the hot syrup into the egg white mixture. Continue beating for 6-8 minutes, until the mixture is very thick. Stir in the nuts and vanilla extract. Pour into a 11 1/2" x 7 1/2" pan which has been sprayed with non-stick stray. Let the candy stand for at least 4 hours, preferably overnight. Turn the candy out onto a board or counter before cutting into squares.

AND MORE CANDY

Makes about 1 pound of candy. Preparation time: about 15 minutes, plus cooling.

1/2 cup chopped walnuts or pecans
3/4 cup light brown sugar
1/4 cup unsalted butter or margarine
6 ounces chocolate bits or chips

Spread the walnuts or pecans evenly over the bottom of a lightly buttered 8" pan. In a medium saucepan, combine the brown sugar and butter. Stirring constantly, bring the mixture to a rolling boil and cook until a candy thermometer reads 270°, about 7 minutes. Pour the mixture over the nuts and sprinkle the chocolate bits evenly over the top. Cover the pan tightly with foil for about 2 minutes. Remove the foil and spread the chocolate evenly. Allow the candy to cool completely before breaking into pieces.

♫ ALLEGRO ♫

Book, music and lyrics by Richard Rodgers
and Oscar Hammerstein, II
Opened October 10, 1947, at the Majestic Theatre

In spite of many imaginative theatrical effects, including a Greek chorus that commented on the reactions of the characters, this first original musical by the authors is one of their least appreciated efforts. Directed and choreographed by Agnes de Mille, *Allegro* presents a serious story, large and universal, in which it is suggested that doctors sometimes lose their integrity as they become rich and successful. Although it boasts some memorable songs -- "A Fellow Needs a Girl," and "The Gentleman Is a Dope" -- Hammerstein admitted that he "overestimated the psychological ability of the audience to identify" with the hero, Dr. Joseph Taylor, Jr., played by John Battles.

Medicine as a business is ridiculed in the Salon scene in Chicago, Act II, where the doctors gather to drink and talk and prescribe nonsense. For the complaint of the patient who cannot sleep, the medical profession agrees:

Broccoli hogwash balderdash
Phoney baloney, tripe and trash.

But perhaps it is not all nonsense. We find distinctly healthful eating in our version of the doctors' remedy.

BROCCOLI HOGWASH BALDERDASH

For a party of 6. Preparation time: about 20 minutes.

1 pound elbow macaroni, penne, ziti or pinwheel pasta
1 tablespoon unsalted butter or margarine
1 tablespoon extra virgin olive oil

1 medium white onion, finely chopped
1 clove garlic, minced
12-15 large fresh mushroom caps, quartered, or 15-30
    small mushroom caps, whole
1/2 teaspoon dried oregano
1 teaspoon dried basil
3 cups beef stock
2 large bunches fresh broccoli, divided into flowerettes
    with about 2" stems
2 tablespoons flour
Shredded mozzarella cheese
Fresh basil, for garnish

Cook the pasta *al dente,* according to package directions. Drain and set aside.

Preheat the oven to 350°. While the pasta cooks, melt the butter in the olive oil in a large skillet over medium-high heat. Add the onion, garlic and mushrooms and sauté until the onion is translucent and the mushrooms are browning. While the onion and mushrooms cook, add the oregano and basil to the beef stock and bring just to a simmer in a small pan.

Place enough water to cover the broccoli in a large saucepan. Bring to a boil over high heat. Add the broccoli, reduce the heat to boil gently and cook, uncovered to preserve the color, about 3 minutes, or until tender-crisp. Drain the broccoli, set aside and keep warm.

Add the flour to the skillet and stir until the flour begins to brown. Add the stock and stir until slightly thickened. If the stock becomes too thick, stir in a bit of water. Add the pasta and toss thoroughly. Add the broccoli and gently toss to distribute evenly. Top with mozzarella, garnish with fresh basil and serve immediately.

♫ SOUTH PACIFIC ♫

Book by Oscar Hammerstein, II, and Joshua Logan
Music by Richard Rodgers
Lyrics by Oscar Hammerstein, II
Opened April 7, 1949, at the Majestic Theatre

Turning James A. Michener's collection of World War II stories, *Tales of the South Pacific*, into a focused stage musical demanded careful selectivity. Finally, the authors agreed upon the tale entitled "Our Heroine," concerned with nurse Nellie Forbush and French planter Emile De Becque, and another tale, "Fo Dollah," depicting the unhappy love affair between Lt. Joe Cable and Liat, a Tonganese girl. By adding an episode with Cable and De Becque on a mission behind enemy lines, they successfully fused the two stories. Mary Martin was chosen to play Nellie, and Ezio Pinza of the Metropolitan Opera Company had already hinted that he wanted to appear in a Broadway musical. He was cast as De Becque. *South Pacific* ran for 1,925 performances and won a Pulitzer Prize in 1950. The music never fails to please -- "Some Enchanted Evening," "I'm in Love with a Wonderful Guy," "Younger Than Springtime," "There is Nothing Like a Dame," "A Cockeyed Optimist."

Nellie, the nurse from Little Rock, Arkansas, and admittedly "immature and incurably green" is swept off her feet in Act I, Scene 1, when she is invited to Emile's plantation home on a lovely island.

> Well, I'm just speechless . . . And that lunch!
> Wild chicken -- I didn't know it was ever wild.

Frankly, neither did we! And for the sake of everyone's good humor, we've substituted a plump domestic fryer in our recipe.

POLYNESIAN "WILD" CHICKEN

For a party of 4.   Preparation time: about 1 hour.

1 fryer, cut into quarters
Melted butter or margarine, for basting

For the sauce:
3 tablespoons cornstarch
1 cup chicken stock
2 tablespoons light soy sauce
2 tablespoons unsalted butter or margarine
1 medium onion, coarsely chopped
1/2 cup coarsely chopped green bell pepper
1/2 cup coarsely chopped red bell pepper
1 cup drained canned pineapple chunks, juice reserved
1/2 cup vinegar
1/2 cup sugar
1/8 teaspoon salt
1 tablespoon grated fresh ginger root
1 orange, unpeeled, coarsely chopped
1 banana, cubed
2 tablespoons grated coconut

Preheat the broiler and broil the chicken, starting with the skin side down, for about 17 minutes on each side, basting frequently with melted butter.

While the chicken broils, blend the cornstarch, 1/2 cup of the chicken stock and the soy sauce. Set aside. In a heavy skillet over medium heat, melt the 2 tablespoons butter. Add the onion and sauté for about 3 minutes. Add the remaining 1/2 cup chicken stock, the bell peppers and pineapple chunks. Increase the heat and bring to a boil. Immediately reduce the heat to simmer, cover and cook for 5 minutes. Add the cornstarch mixture, vinegar, reserved pineapple juice, sugar, salt and ginger root. Raise the heat to boil and stir constantly until the sauce thickens.

Remove the chicken from the broiler. Adjust the oven to bake at 350°. Arrange the chicken in a single layer in a baking dish that has been sprayed with non-stick spray. Around the chicken, arrange the orange and banana pieces. Sprinkle evenly with the coconut. Pour the sauce over the chicken and fruit and bake for 10-12 minutes. Serve hot with boiled white rice or Chinese noodles.

♫

As part of the holiday show performed on the G.I. stage in Act II, Scene 3, the nurses close their act with a song.

    Nurses: We hope you liked us,
          And hope that when you leave your seat and run
          Down to the Mess Hall
          You'll enjoy your dinner, each and every one.
    Nellie: Enjoy your turkey!

For Thanksgiving Turkey, see the recipe on page 133.

38

♫ LOST IN THE STARS ♫

Book and lyrics by Maxwell Anderson
Music by Kurt Weill
Opened October 30, 1949, at the Music Box Theatre

This musical adaptation of Alan Paton's novel, *Cry, the Beloved Country*, reunited the team of Anderson and Weill, who, eleven years earlier, had written *Knickerbocker Holiday*.

Maxwell Anderson is remembered as a theorist -- *The Essence of Tragedy* (1939) -- and a thought-provoking playwright whose range of work into politics, anti-war activity, contemporary events and historical figures suggests the probing nature of his mind. He was particularly interested in language in the theatre and in writing poetic drama. *Elizabeth the Queen* excited critics in 1930, and *Winterset* (1935) received the first Drama Critics Circle Award.

Of this, Kurt Weill's last work (he died the next year at the age of fifty) Weill said that he wanted to project a "message of hope that people, through a personal approach, will solve whatever racial problems exist." A complete man of the theatre, Weill believed that America would "develop a musical-dramatic form" that would not be called "opera" but would grow from and remain a part of "Broadway theatre." Always a serious composer, he felt sympathy for contemporary man: "I write for today."

Lost in the Stars became part of the New York City Opera Company's repertory, and a major revival in 1972 at the Imperial Theatre received two Tony Awards.

At a dive in Shanty Town, Linda sings, "Who'll Buy?"

Who'll buy/My juicy rutabagas?
Who'll buy/My yellow corn?

Who'll buy asparagus or carrots or potatoes?
Who wants my peppers and my ginger and tomatoes,
The best you bit into/Since you were born?

We'll buy, Linda! And this is the way we'll cook some of your offerings.

RUTABAGAS & POTATOES

For a party of 6.   Preparation time: about 1 hour.

2 medium rutabagas, peeled and diced
2 medium Irish potatoes, peeled and diced
2 tablespoons unsalted butter or margarine
2 tablespoons (or more) non-fat sour cream
Salt and freshly ground black pepper, to taste
1/4 cup chopped fresh parsley or Italian parsley
Sprigs of fresh parsley or Italian parsley, for garnish

In a saucepan, bring to a boil over high heat enough water to cover the rutabagas. Add the rutabagas and reduce the heat so that the water maintains the boil but does not boil over. Cook, uncovered, until tender, about 25 minutes.

Meanwhile, in another saucepan, repeat the above process with the potatoes, cooking until tender, about 20 minutes.

Drain the rutabagas and potatoes and toss together in a large mixing bowl. Add the butter and 2 tablespoons sour cream and mash until the mixture is smooth. Add more sour cream if the mixture seems too dry. Season with salt and pepper, to taste. Sprinkle with the chopped parsley, garnish with the fresh parsley and serve very warm.

A recipe for corn-on-the-cob appears on page 11.   For asparagus soup, see page 183.

♫ CALL ME MADAM ♫

Book by Howard Lindsay and Russel Crouse
Music and lyrics by Irving Berlin
Opened October 12, 1950, at the Imperial Theatre

Inspired by President Harry Truman's appointment of Washington's popular party-giver Perle Mesta to the post of U.S. Ambassador to Luxembourg, the authors light-heartedly spoofed American politics and the American people. Described by Howard Lindsay as "the most American American," Ethel Merman dazzled audiences as Mrs. Sally Adams, newly appointed ambassadress to Lichtenberg and clearly identifiable as "The Hostess with the Mostes' on the Ball." As the abrasive yet amiable dynamo who could not take "No" for an answer, Merman combined Irving Berlin's enthusiasm for America with the patriotic vigor of George M. Cohan and the brassy self-indulgence of Perle Mesta.

A sympathetic undercurrent of romantic love in *Call Me Madam* is revealed in songs such as "It's a Lovely Day Today," and "You're Just in Love." A specialty number, "They Like Ike," soon became a campaign song and an effective slogan through the simple change of the pronoun: "I Like Ike" appeared on millions of lapel buttons across the country. The show ran for 644 performances in New York and so suited Ethel Merman that she starred as Sally Adams in the 1953 film version, the only stage role she repeated on the screen.

With a hostess as its heroine, *Call Me Madam* naturally has dance numbers. And in them we find foods we enjoy.

The Washington Square Dance is square.
Bow to your partners . . .
Now duck for the oyster
Dig for the clam
But do your digging for Uncle Sam.

41

WASHINGTON SQUARE DANCE FRIED OYSTERS

For a party of 6-8.   Preparation time: about 20 minutes.

Canola or safflower oil, for deep frying
4 dozen oysters, shucked and well drained
2 cups finely ground cracker crumbs
4-6 eggs, well beaten

Heat the oil in the deep fryer.   Roll the oysters in the cracker crumbs, coating evenly, dip into the beaten eggs, then again into the crumbs.   Place the oysters in a wire basket, plunge them into the hot oil and fry until golden brown and crisp. Serve immediately.

UNCLE SAM'S CLAMS
(ALSO KNOWN AS STEAMERS)

For a party of 6-8.   Preparation time: about 15 minutes.

4 dozen soft-shell clams
Lemon wedges, for garnish
Clarified unsalted butter, for dipping (see page 28)

Scrub the clams thoroughly and bathe them in several washes of water.   Arrange the clams closely in the top of a steamer pan and add 1/2" of water to the pan. (You may need to use more than one pan or steam the clams in batches.)   Cover the steamer pan tightly and steam over moderate heat just until the clams open, about 5-10 minutes.   Discard any unopened clams; reserve the cooking liquid.   Serve the clams in individual bowls, garnished with the lemon wedges and accompanied by small bowls of clarified butter.   Before dipping into the butter, remove any sand by dipping each clam into a bowl of the cooking liquid.   Do not attempt to eat the neck sheath! Your guests will thank you if you provide plenty of napkins and, perhaps, warm washcloths.

♫ GUYS AND DOLLS ♫

Book by Jo Swerling and Abe Burrows
Music and lyrics by Frank Loesser
Opened March 24, 1950, at the Forty-Sixth Street Theatre

Much of the success of this tightly coordinated musical rests upon the ability of Frank Loesser to catch the appealing variety and ambivalence of the Damon Runyon characters who brightened up Broadway during the 1930s. Presumably, Loesser was inspired by people he had actually known while working as a singer and pianist at the Back Drop, a 52nd Street night club. Featuring Vivian Blaine as Adelaide, a night club singer, and Sam Levine as Nathan Detroit, her fiancé, as well as Robert Alda, B. S. Pully, Stubby Kaye and Isabel Bigley, *Guys and Dolls* ran for 1,200 performances. It was successfully revived in 1976 with an all-black cast and again in 1992 with Faith Prince and Nathan Lane.

Horse racing, crap games, night club romance and, of course, love in its many attitudes are part of the life of Broadway's "guys and dolls." For example, "If I Were a Bell," what would I do?

> Or if I were a goose I'd be cooked
> Ask me how do I feel
> Ask me now that we're fondly caressing,
> Pal, if I were a salad I know
> I'd be splashing my dressing.

SPLASHING DRESSING SALAD

For a party of 6-8. Preparation time: about 25 minutes, plus chilling.

8 small new potatoes, boiled in their jackets and diced
1 1/2 cups fresh young green beans, steamed until
    tender-crisp

1 cup fresh young wax beans, steamed until tender-crisp
1 cup cooked kidney beans, well drained
1/4 cup (or more) extra virgin olive oil
1/4 cup fresh Italian parsley, finely chopped
1/4 cup fresh basil leaves, finely chopped
Salt and freshly ground black pepper, to taste
Grated Romano cheese
Sprigs of fresh Italian parsley or fresh basil, for garnish

In a large bowl, combine the potatoes, beans, oil, chopped parsley and chopped basil. Add the salt and pepper. Toss well, adding more oil if needed to coat thoroughly. Chill for 1-3 hours. Sprinkle with the cheese and garnish with the fresh parsley or basil.

♫

If Nathan Detroit has his problems, Adelaide has an answer:

Marry the man today
Handle it meek and gently,
Marry the man today and train him subsequently.
Carefully expose him to domestic life,
And if he ever tries to stray from you
Have a pot roast, Have a headache, Have a baby,
Have two, six, nine, Stop, But
Marry the man today.

For a New York Pot Roast that will keep all the guys and dolls around your house from straying, see the recipe on page 88.

♬ THE KING AND I ♬

Book, music and lyrics by Richard Rodgers
and Oscar Hammerstein, II
Opened March 29, 1951, at the St. James Theatre

Maynard Landon's book, *Anna and the King of Siam*, so impressed Gertrude Lawrence that she persuaded Rodgers and Hammerstein to adapt it as a musical for her. Because the relationship between the Victorian English school teacher and her rather forbidding royal employer denied the writers the possibility of using such familiar phrases as "I love you," they were doubly challenged to present their story through song and dance. The King's stubborn, questioning nature is revealed in his song, "A Puzzlement," and explained in Lady Thiang's "Something Wonderful." Jerome Robbins' Siamese version of *Uncle Tom's Cabin*, presented as a play-within-the-play entitled "The Small House of Uncle Thomas," and the rousing romantic polka number, "Shall We Dance?" are show-stoppers.

For his performance as the King, later winning him an Academy Award for Best Actor in the film version, Yul Brynner became a full-fledged star. Gertrude Lawrence, however, did not see *The King and I* finish its run of 1,246 performances: she died on September 6, 1952.

The action takes place in and around the King's palace in Bangkok, Siam, in the early 1860's. One Western visitor is a British Diplomat, Sir Edward Ramsey, an old friend of Anna. For the occasion (Act I, Scene 6) the King, determined to refute recent charges that he is a "barbarian," commands that a fine dinner be served, featuring "eminent European dishes." By Act II, Scene 1, the dinner has taken place, but we have not been told what was served. We have, therefore, provided a trio of "eminent" French dishes certain to refute any claims that those who serve them are anything but individuals of sophistication and refinement.

SOUPE A L'OIGNON

For a party of 8.   Preparation time: about 40 minutes.

1/2 cup unsalted butter or margarine
8 medium onions, thinly sliced
2 tablespoons flour
1/2 teaspoon salt
Freshly ground black pepper, to taste
2 quarts beef stock
1 loaf French bread, cut into 8 slices
1/2 cup grated Parmesan cheese
1/2 cup grated Gruyere cheese

In a large skillet melt the butter over medium heat. Add the onions and sauté, stirring occasionally, until golden. Stir in the flour and cook until it begins to brown. Add the salt and pepper. Add the stock, a bit at a time, stirring constantly. Raise the heat to bring the soup just to a boil, immediately lower the heat to simmer, partially cover the pan and cook for about 20 minutes.

While the soup simmers, toast the bread slices and preheat the broiler.   Arrange the toasted bread in an oven-proof soup tureen or individual serving bowls. Sprinkle the Parmesan cheese evenly over the bread. Pour the soup over the bread and top with the Gruyere cheese. Broil until the cheese begins to melt. Serve immediately.

RAGOÛT DE BOEUF

For a party of 8.   Preparation time: about 2 hours and 30 minutes.

1/3 cup (or more) flour
1 1/2 teaspoons salt

1/2 teaspoon freshly ground black pepper
3 pounds stew beef, cut into 1 1/2" chunks
3 tablespoons corn, canola or safflower oil
2 small stalks celery, with leaves
4-5 sprigs fresh parsley
1 bay leaf
2-3 sprigs fresh thyme
1 large onion
6 whole cloves
8 small new potatoes
3 medium carrots, sliced diagonally into 2" pieces
4-5 stalks celery, without leaves, cut into 1 1/2" pieces
10 ounces frozen peas
1/2 pound fresh mushrooms, trimmed and sliced

In a paper or plastic bag, combine the flour, 1 teaspoon of salt and the pepper. Add the beef and shake the bag to coat the meat evenly. Reserve the remaining flour. Heat the oil in a very large skillet over medium-high heat, add the beef and cook until evenly browned on all sides. Reduce the heat slightly, pour off any excess fat and add 3 cups of water to the skillet.

Make a *bouquet garni:* tie together the celery stalks with leaves, parsley, bay leaf and thyme. Add the *bouquet garni* to the skillet. Stud the onion with the cloves and add to the skillet. Reduce the heat to simmer, cover tightly and cook for 1 hour. Remove the *bouquet garni* and the onion.

Add the new potatoes, carrots and cut celery and cook, uncovered, about 45 minutes. Add the peas, mushrooms and the remaining 1/2 teaspoon salt. Cover and cook for about 15 minutes, or until the meat is very tender. Remove the meat and vegetables to a heated bowl. Add as much of the reserved flour as needed to the cooking liquid, a bit at a time, stirring constantly, until the mixture thickens. Pour the liquid over the meat and vegetables and serve immediately with French bread (see page 177).

MOUSSE AU CHOCOLAT

For a party of 8.   Preparation time: about 45 minutes, plus chilling.

6 ounces semisweet chocolate
6 eggs, separated
6 tablespoons unsalted butter
3 tablespoons Grand Marnier or 1 1/2 teaspoons pure
    vanilla extract
1/3 cup sugar
Whipped cream, for topping

In a large saucepan, cover the chocolate with about 2" of very hot water, cover and let stand until the chocolate is softened, about 5 minutes. Carefully pour off the water. With a wire whisk, stir in the egg yolks, one at a time. Place the saucepan over low heat and cook until the mixture thickens. Remove the pan from the heat and blend in the butter, a tablespoon at a time. Blend in the Grand Marnier. Allow the mixture to cool for a few minutes.

While the mixture cools, beat the egg whites until soft peaks form. Add the sugar, a tablespoon at a time. Beat until stiff peaks form.

Pour the chocolate mixture into a large mixing bowl. With the wire whisk, beat in 1/4 of the egg whites. With a rubber spatula, gently fold in the remaining egg whites. Pour the mixture into individual serving glasses or bowls and chill for 1 hour. Top with whipped cream and serve immediately.

♫ WONDERFUL TOWN ♫

Book by Joseph Fields and Jerome Chodorov
Music by Leonard Bernstein
Lyrics by Betty Comden and Adolph Green
Opened February 25, 1953, at the Winter Garden Theatre

Leonard Bernstein's tremendous enthusiam for "The Thirties, My God, those were the years!" pushed a reluctant Comden and Green to complete this musical based on Fields and Chodorov's Broadway hit play of 1940, *My Sister Eileen*. Exploiting the adventures of two sisters -- Ruth, a writer, and Eileen, an actress -- who come to New York to further their careers, *Wonderful Town* is a slight and nostalgic musical reflecting Greenwich Village life during the mid-Thirties. Its most memorable features were the performances of Rosalind Russell, who, at age forty-five, played older sister Ruth with an exuberance that hypnotized audiences, and Edith (later known as Edie) Adams, who sparkled as Eileen.

The culinary adventures of the sisters in New Work were typical of farce. Incongruities in selection and devastating consequences usually get a laugh. Consider Act I, Scene 3:

> Eileen: Today I had a pimiento sandwich, a tomato surprise, and a giant double malt -- with a marble cake.

Tomato surprise?? We'll stick with marble cake.

EILEEN'S MARBLE CAKE

1 box white cake mix
3 egg whites
2 tablespoons canola or safflower oil
1/3 cup baking cocoa
1/4 cup confectioners sugar

Preheat the oven to 350°. Grease and flour 2 8" cake pans. In a large bowl, mix the cake mix, egg whites and oil with 1 1/3 cups of water, with a mixer on low speed, until moistened. Beat on medium speed for 2 minutes. Remove 1 cup of the mixture to another bowl and add to it the cocoa, confectioners sugar and 2 tablespoons of water. Mix thoroughly. Pour 1/2 of the first mixture into each pan. Gently swirl 1/2 of the second mixture into each pan, being careful not to blend the two mixtures. Bake for about 30 minutes, or until a toothpick inserted into the center of the cake comes out clean. Cool in the pans on racks for 5 minutes. Remove from the pans and cool completely before frosting.

♫

And in Act I, Scene 6 . . .

> Eileen: What've we got for dinner, Ruth?
> Ruth: What do you think? Spaghetti and meat balls.
> Eileen: Haven't we polished that off yet? We've had it all week.
> Ruth (flatly): It closes tonight.

Later, the audience hears a crash, as Eileen spills the spaghetti and meatballs on the kitchen floor. We hope your dish makes it to the table and doesn't last all week!

SPAGHETTI AND MEATBALLS

For a party of 4-6. Preparation time: 2 hours, including simmering.

For the sauce:
1 tablespoon extra virgin olive oil
1 medium onion, chopped
1-2 cloves garlic, chopped
1 28-ounce can crushed or ground tomatoes in their liquid

1 teaspoon dried basil
1 teaspoon dried oregano
2 teaspoons dried Italian parsley
1 bay leaf
Freshly grated Romano or Parmesan cheese

For the meatballs:
1 medium onion, finely minced
1-2 cloves garlic, finely minced
Approximately 1 3/4 pounds extra lean ground beef
2 teaspoons dried basil
1 teaspoon dried oregano
1 teaspoon dried Italian parsley
1 teaspoon Worcestershire sauce
1-2 (or more) egg whites
1/4 - 1/2 cup (or more) fine cracker crumbs

1 1/2 pounds uncooked spaghetti.

Make the sauce: In a large skillet, heat the oil over medium-low heat. Add the onion and sauté until translucent. Add the garlic and continue sautéing for about 3 minutes. Add the tomatoes and their liquid, the basil, oregano, Italian parsley and bay leaf. Raise the heat to bring the sauce to a boil. Immediately reduce the heat to simmer, cover and cook for at least 1 hour (preferably longer).

Make the meatballs: If broiling, preheat the broiler. In a large bowl, using your hands, combine all the ingredients and mix until thoroughly combined. Form into about 20 1 1/2" balls. If the mixture is too dry to form into balls, add another egg white and mix thoroughly. If the mixture is too moist, mix in an additional 1/4 cup cracker crumbs.

Cook the meatballs in the broiler (for less fat) for about 7 minutes on each side; or skillet fry in extra virgin olive oil, turning to brown evenly on all sides, for about 15 minutes. If skillet frying, drain the meatballs well and allow them to stand for a few minutes on several folds of paper toweling, turning to blot evenly.

When the sauce has cooked for 1 hour or more, add the meatballs and simmer for 12-15 minutes. Remove the bay leaf. While the meatballs simmer in the sauce, cook the spaghetti *al dente,* according to package directions.

Spoon the sauce and meatballs over the spaghetti, top with cheese and serve immediately with crusty Italian bread and a good California burgundy.

♫ ME AND JULIET ♫

Book, music and lyrics by Richard Rodgers
and Oscar Hammerstein, II
Opened March 28, 1953, at the Majestic Theatre

One critic described *Me and Juliet* as Rodgers and Hammerstein's valentine to show business. Having been in love with the theatre since early youth, the two men left their exotic productions of *South Pacific* and *The King and I* to write a musical melodrama of backstage love. Isabel Bigley, Bill Hayes and Joan McCracken led the cast of young actors, but the show ran for only forty-five weeks -- a weak showing for a Rodgers and Hammerstein effort.

As the curtain rises in Act I, a chorus girl sits at the stage manager's desk and sings to herself:

> How does it all start -- this boy/girl world!
> You are shy and uncertain
> But he pleads and you yield,
> And you don't have an inkling
> That you're signed and sealed.
> > By merely telling someone you'd be glad to partake
> > Of French fried potatoes and a T-Bone steak.
> > That's the way it happens,
> > That's the way it happens,
> > That's the way it happened to me!

To evoke memories, check out the steak and fries!

T-BONE STEAK

For a party of 6. Preparation time: about 10 minutes.

6 T-bone steaks, 1 1/2" - 2" thick

About 1 hour before cooking, remove the steaks from the refrigerator.

Preheat the broiler. Place the steaks on a broiling grid over a shallow broiling pan, both of which have been sprayed with non-stick spray. If the steaks are 1 1/2" thick, place them 3" from the heat source and broil, turning once, for about 7 minutes on each side for rare, 8 minutes on each side for medium. If steaks are 2" thick, place them 4" from the heat source and broil for about 9 minutes per side for rare and 10 minutes per side for medium.

FRENCH FRIED POTATOES

For a party of 6.   Preparation time: about 30 minutes.

Vegetable oil, for deep frying
3 large, mature potatoes, peeled and sliced into 2 1/4" strips
    about 3/8" thick

Heat the oil to 300°-330° in a deep fryer. Drop in the potato strips, about 1 potato at a time, and cook for 2 minutes, or until the potatoes stop sputtering. Drain the strips on several folds of paper toweling. Cool for 5 minutes. Raise the heat of the oil to 365°. Place the potato strips in a frying basket and submerge in the oil for about 3 minutes, or until golden brown. Drain on paper towels and serve, immediately, uncovered, in a basket lined with a napkin.

♫ THE GOLDEN APPLE ♫

Book by John Latouche   Music by Jerome Moross
Opened March 11, 1954, at the Phoenix Theatre

Kaye Ballard as Helen and Jonathan Lucas as Paris starred in this retelling of the Judgment of Paris Myth. The setting is Washington State's Mount Olympus during the first decade of the twentieth century, following the return of Ulysses from the Spanish-American War. *The Golden Apple* won the Drama Critics' Circle Award for Best Musical and subsequently ran for 125 performances at Broadway's Alvin Theatre.

At a picnic and a fair to celebrate the soldiers' homecoming, Mother Hare announces a "golden apple"--

As the general prize
For the one who makes
The very best cakes and pies.
[Paris, a traveling man, will be the judge.]

Minerva: I thought I'd bake a seven-layer cake
    Just to prove I'm feminine.
Lovey Mars: This pie I made has mincemeat filling
    With their names spelt out in choc-o-late!
Mrs. Juniper: My angel food has won a prize
    At every fair for twenty years.

Paris gives the "golden apple" to Lovey Mars, who offers him "A love that will not die." Unfortunately, she also introduces him to Helen, with consequences that are dire indeed. Meanwhile, however, we will introduce you to some prize-winning recipes.

LOVEY MARS' MINCEMEAT PIE

For a party of 6-8.   Preparation time: about 1 hour.

For the crust:
1 teaspoon vinegar
1/2 cup milk
1 cup vegetable shortening
2 cups unbleached flour

For the filling:
1/4 cup lean ground beef
1/4 cup lean ground pork
1 1/2 cups chopped apples
1/2 cup golden raisins
2 tablespoons melted unsalted butter or margarine
1/8 teaspoon salt
1 teaspoon cinnamon
1/4 teaspoon ground cloves
1 tablespoon molasses
2/3 cup sugar
2 tablespoons vinegar

Preheat the oven to 425°.   In a small bowl, stir the vinegar into the milk.   Set aside.   In a large bowl, cut the shortening into the flour, add the milk and, with well floured hands, work into a sticky dough -- very sticky! Divide the dough into 2 balls. On a well floured surface, roll out the first ball into a circle 1/8" thick. Place in a greased pie pan. Roll out the other ball into a circle 1/8" thick.

In another large bowl, combine the beef, pork, apples, raisins, butter, salt, cinnamon, cloves, molasses, sugar, vinegar and 2 tablespoons of cold water. Stir well. Spread the mixture in the pie pan, top the pie with the second crust and seal the edges with your fingers or a fork. Pierce the top crust several times with the fork, or cut a decorative design. Bake for 15 minutes. Reduce the heat to 350° and bake for 15 minutes more.

Note: We also like the commercial mincemeats, although -- or perhaps because -- they do not contain any meat! If you agree, substitute a large jar of mincemeat, with a tablespoon or two of rum added, if you wish, for our recipe for filling.

MRS. JUNIPER'S ANGEL FOOD CAKE

For a party of 10-12.   Preparation time: about 1 hour, plus standing.

1 dozen egg whites
1 1/2 teaspoons cream of tartar
1/8 teaspoon salt
1 1/2 teaspoons vanilla extract
1/2 teaspoon almond extract
1 cup granulated sugar
1 cup unbleached flour
1 1/4 cups confectioners sugar

Place the egg whites in a very large mixing bowl and let stand at room temperature for 1 hour.

Preheat the oven to 375°.   Add the cream of tartar, salt, vanilla extract and almond extract to the egg whites. Beat with a mixer at high speed until very stiff but not dry. Beat in the granulated sugar, 1 or 2 tablespoons at a time. Continue beating until stiff peaks form.

In another bowl, sift together the flour and confectioners sugar. Sift 3 times. Sift about 1/4 of this mixture at a time over the meringue and fold in gently. Spread the batter evenly into a well greased 10" tube pan and bake for 30-35 minutes. Invert the pan and allow the cake to cool 10 minutes before removing from the pan.

♫ THE PAJAMA GAME ♫

Book by George Abbott and Richard Bissell
Music and lyrics by Richard Adler and Jerry Ross
Opened May 13, 1954, at the St. James Theatre

Adler and Ross -- "two young Loessers," according to Leonard Bernstein -- were the bright, new song-writing team of the decade. Ross once said that they wrote for the "man in the street," an approach more ambitiously stated by Adler as expressing "universal truths in colloquial terms." In *The Pajama Game*, based on Richard Bissell's novel, *7 1/2 Cents*, they set up fun and romance in the Sleep Tite pajama factory, between the superintendent played by John Raitt and a labor union agitator played by Janis Paige. Eddie Foy, Jr., was part of the supercilious management, and Carol Haney danced the sensational "Steam Heat," created by Bob Fosse.

Much of the action in Act I revolves around the Annual Picnic of the Associated Garment Makers, Local 243. En route to the picnic, Moe makes an announcement:

> Well, I'll have to make an announcement about the mixup. It seems there ain't going to be enough baked beans to go around. . . . But there's plenty of potato salad . . . so them that doesn't care for beans can go heavily on the potato salad and vice versa.

Be warned and prepare enough beans. And vice versa.

LOCAL 243 BAKED BEANS

For a party of 6. Preparation time: about 7 hours.

3 cups dried beans
1 small white onion
1/2 pound salt pork, scored
1/4 cup molasses

1/4 cup brown sugar
1 teaspoon dry mustard
1/2 teaspoon salt
1/4 teaspoon freshly ground black pepper

In a large saucepan, cover the beans with cold water and bring to a boil over high heat. Immediately reduce the heat to simmer and cook for 5 minutes. Drain and rinse the beans.

Preheat the oven to 400°. Place the whole onion and the salt pork in the bottom of an oven-proof pot and cover with the beans. In a small bowl, mix together the molasses, brown sugar, dry mustard, salt and pepper and a little water. Add the mixture to the beans, along with enough water to cover the beans. Cover and bake until the beans begin to boil. Reduce the heat to 325°. Bake for 3 hours, adding water if necessary. Remove the cover and bake for 3 hours more. Remove the onion. Serve the beans hot.

GARMENT MAKERS' POTATO SALAD

For a party of 6-8. Preparation time: about 30 minutes, plus chilling.

6 medium potatoes, peeled
2/3 cup mayonnaise
1-2 teaspoons Dijon mustard
3 tablespoons vinegar
Sugar, to taste
1 cup heavy cream
Salt and freshly ground black pepper, to taste
1 small onion, chopped
1 cup frozen peas, thawed
1 stalk celery, chopped
1 hard boiled egg, sliced
Paprika

Bring enough water to cover the potatoes to a rapid boil in a large saucepan. Add the potatoes and cook until tender, about 20-25 minutes. Allow to cool enough to handle. Meanwhile, in a large bowl, mix the mayonnaise, mustard, vinegar and sugar. Whip the cream and gently fold into the mayonnaise mixture. Dice the potatoes, add the salt and pepper and toss with the onion, peas and celery. Fold the potato mixture into the cream mixture. Chill well. Top with the egg slices and sprinkle with the paprika. Serve immediately.

♫

One of the most memorable scenes in *The Pajama Game* takes place in Act II, in the low riverfront dive identified by a name that, because of a song, became a household word during the mid-Fifties.

> Just knock three times and whisper low
> That you and I were sent by Joe
> Then strike a match and you will know
> You're in Hernando's Hideaway.
> [Where they serve chop suey -- see page 78.]

Olé!

♫ DAMN YANKEES ♫

Book by George Abbott and Douglass Wallop
Music and lyrics by Richard Adler and Jerry Ross
Opened May 5, 1955, at the Forty-Sixth Street Theatre

This baseball fantasy takes place in Washington, D.C., where the Devil, a Mr. Applegate who "doesn't want to see the Damn Yankees win again," presumably operates openly and without fear. To insure his pact with baseball player Joe Hardy, Applegate, played by Ray Walston, engages Lola, a beautiful redhead, played by Gwen Verdon in her first starring role. As her song reveals, "Whatever Lola Wants, Lola Gets." With George Abbott's sprightly directing, *Damn Yankees* ran for 1,019 performances.

Having explained to Applegate that she will give Joe Hardy her "standard vampire treatment," Lola is ready for her first meeting with Joe in Act I, Scene 8. Applegate, Devil that he is, introduces them and then decides to leave them alone and go out for a hot dog. It is that hot dog that we hope you will enjoy -- with all the zing and zest that a red-headed temptress and a remorseless devil can inspire.

THE DEVIL'S HOT DOG

For a party of 8, with extra chili for all.   Preparation time: 1 hour or more, including simmering.

For the chili:
1 tablespoon extra virgin olive oil
1 pound extra lean ground beef
3 links hot Italian sausage (about 9 ounces), skin removed, coarsely chopped
1 medium onion, finely chopped
1-3 cloves garlic, finely chopped

61

1-2 tablespoons (or more, to taste) chili powder
2 teaspoons (or more) ground cumin
A pinch (or more) dried red pepper flakes
A generous grating fresh black pepper
1/2 teaspoon (or more) chopped pickled jalapeños
1 28-ounce can crushed or ground tomatoes in their liquid

For the hot dogs:
8 beef franks
8 hot dog buns
Dijon mustard
Sweet pickle relish
4-6 scallions, chopped into 1/8" rounds
1 red bell pepper, seeds and membranes removed, finely
    chopped
Shredded cheddar cheese

Make the chili: In a large skillet, heat the olive oil over medium heat. Add the beef and sausage and sauté for about 5 minutes, stirring and blending with a fork to mix well. Add the onion and garlic and cook until the onion is translucent. Stir in the chili powder, cumin, red pepper flakes and black pepper. Add the jalapeños and tomatoes. Bring to a boil. Immediately reduce the heat to simmer, cover and cook for at least 30 minutes (preferably 1 hour or more).

At this point, a taste test is in order: chili powder, cumin, red pepper flakes, fresh black pepper and/or jalapeños may be added until the desired seasoning is reached. (But please, don't add salt!) Cover and simmer for at least 15 minutes after adding more spices.

Make the hot dogs: When the chili is almost ready, steam or grill the franks. Open the buns and spread liberally with the mustard and relish. Place the franks in the buns, spoon the chili generously over the franks, top with the scallions and red bell pepper and sprinkle with the cheese. Serve immediately. (You may want to provide forks, and you surely will want plenty of napkins ready-to-hand -- these hot dogs make a devil of a mess!)

♫ **MY FAIR LADY** ♫

Adaptation and lyrics by Alan Jay Lerner
Music by Frederick Loewe
Opened March 15, 1956, at the Mark Hellinger Theatre

A record breaker for its time -- with gross receipts of $10 million and with 2,717 performances in New York and 228 in London -- *My Fair Lady* is another landmark in the progress of American musical theatre. At first opposed to the idea of a musical version of his play, *Pygmalion* (1914), G. B. Shaw eventually relented. After his death in 1950, Lerner and Loewe undertook an adaptation but struggled to find the proper approach, finally achieving it in those marvelous songs that help structure the musical, move the plot and reveal the characters. There is Professor Henry Higgins (Rex Harrison) with "Why Can't the English?," "I'm an Ordinary Man" and "A Hymn to Him"; there is Eliza Doolittle (Julie Andrews) with "Wouldn't It Be Loverly?," "Just You Wait" and "I Could Have Danced All Night"; there is Alfred Doolittle (Stanley Holloway) with "With a Little Bit of Luck" and "Get Me to the Church on Time." And, of course, there is the wonderfully dramatic scene that comes to a climax with "The Rain in Spain Stays Mainly in the Plain."

In Act, II, Scene 5, the two gentlemen -- Higgins and Colonel Pickering -- prepare Eliza, in their determined and somewhat heartless fashion, for their grand wager:

Pickering: The strawberry tarts are delicious. And did you try the pline cake?

Before the eyes of Eliza, who is very hungry, Higgins responds by giving the last of the strawberry tarts to the bird in the cage. Effective inspiration for Eliza, perhaps, but not for us. Our tarts are strictly for human enjoyment, and so is our version of pline cake!

STRAWBERRY TARTS

For a party of 8.   Preparation time: about 35 minutes.

1/2 cup unsalted butter or margarine, softened
1/2 cup firmly packed light brown sugar
1 egg or 2 ounces egg substitute
1 1/2 cups flour
1/4 teaspoon baking powder
1/8 teaspoon (or less) salt
1/2 teaspoon pure vanilla extract
3 tablespoons strawberry jam or preserves

Preheat the oven to 350°.   In a large bowl, cream the
butter and sugar. Add the egg and beat well. Sift in the
flour, baking powder and salt and add the vanilla extract.
Mix well. Divide the dough into 16 equal portions, roll
out into circles and press into small, well greased muffin
cups. Place a little more than 1/2 teaspoon of the jam in
the center of each tart. Bake for 15 minutes. Cool for a
few minutes before removing from the pans.

PLINE CAKE

For a party of 12-16.   Preparation time: about 1 hour and
30 minutes, plus cooling.

3 cups sugar
1 cup unsalted butter or margarine
1/2 cup vegetable shortening
5 eggs or 10 ounces egg substitute
1 teaspoon pura vanilla extract
1 teaspoon pure lemon or almond extract
3 cups plus 5 tablespoons flour
1/2 teaspoon baking powder
1 cup milk

In a large bowl, cream the sugar, butter and shortening.
Beat in the eggs and extracts. In another bowl, sift together

the flour and baking powder. Add the flour mixture alternately with the milk to the sugar mixture, beating well after each addition. Pour the batter into a well greased and floured tube pan. Place the pan in a cold oven, turn the heat to 340° and bake for 1 hour and 15 minutes. Cool in the pan on a rack.

♫ BELLS ARE RINGING ♫

Book and lyrics by Betty Comden and Adolph Green
Music by Jule Styne
Opened November 29, 1956, at the Shubert Theatre

Having worked with Judy Holliday in their satirical night club act, Comden and Green wrote *Bells Are Ringing* as a vehicle for her talent for creating a broad range of characters. Ella Peterson, Holliday's first musical role, is the meddlesome switchboard operator who, working for "Susanswerphone" answering service, has a wonderful opportunity to involve herself in the lives of her clients. *Bells Are Ringing* also marked the Broadway debut of Sydney Chaplin, who played Jeff Moss, the playwright with whom Ella eventually falls in love.

A firm believer in complete independence, Jeff expresses his opinions in song in Act I, Scene 2:

> I don't need anyone and no one needs me.
> No need for anyone to help me
> Mix martinis, roast the wienies, bake the blinis
> Now that I'm free.

Other views will be expressed on this subject before the end of the musical, but before these complications arise, let's bake the blinis.

JEFF'S BLINIS

For a party of 8. Preparation time: about 3 hours and 30 minutes, including rising.

2 cups milk
1 cake compressed yeast
2 cups sifted flour
1 tablespoon sugar
3 egg yolks

1 tablespoon melted unsalted butter or margarine
1/2 teaspoon salt
3 egg whites
1/2 cup caviar
1/2 cup sour cream or non-fat sour cream

Scald the milk, place in a large bowl and allow to cool to 85°. Add the yeast and dissolve. Add 1 1/2 cups of flour and the sugar and stir until well blended. Cover and set the bowl in a warm place for about 1 1/2 hours. In another bowl, combine the egg yolks and melted butter and beat until blended. Add the remaining flour and the salt and beat this mixture into the yeast dough. Allow the dough to rise again until almost doubled in bulk, about 1 1/2 hours. Whip the egg whites until stiff but not dry and fold into the batter. Let the batter stand about 10 minutes. Heat a griddle to the point that a drop of cold water bounces and sputters on the surface, and cook the batter in small portions until lightly brown, turning once. Place a heaping tablespoon of caviar in the center of each blini, roll and serve topped with sour cream.

♫

During a party at Larry Hasting's penthouse apartment in Act II, Scene 3, the name dropping gets out of control -- to Ella's disgust.

> Girl: Dined with Jean, Le Pavillon
>   Then flew right on to St. Mark's Pizza.
> Man: Took a group for onion soup at dawn to Les
>   Halles -- It never shuts --
> Ella: Like Chock-Full-O'-Nuts!

For Onion Soup, see the recipe on page 46.

♫ NEW GIRL IN TOWN ♫

Book by George Abbott   Music and lyrics by Bob Merrill
Opened May 14, 1957, at the Forty-Sixth Street Theatre

As critics noted, it was "uphill work" to twist the incest, prostitution and despair of Eugene O'Neill's *Anna Christie*, the source for *New Girl in Town*, into a zingy and zestful musical. The transformation was particularly hectic for Abbott and Merrill, and what finally appeared was more a tribute to Gwen Verdon as Anna and Thelma Ritter as Marthy than to O'Neill. A run of 431 performances, however, vindicated the work.

Dances such as "At the Check Apron Ball" showed Gwen Verdon at her best and suggested the waterfront atmosphere of New York just after the turn of the century. For the show-stopper at the close of Act I, an alderman sings of Angelo Galoopy, a barber from Italy who came to New York and was teased about his dress and appearance:

Angelo would bet a bowlful of spaghetti,
He was just as flashy as they, he'd say:
    When I get dressed in all my best,
    There ain't no flies on me.

Nor, we hope, on the spaghetti!   A recipe for spaghetti appears on page 50.

By Act II, Scene 5, things have changed. Anna is working on a farm on Staten Island, and a reformed Marthy, in a Seamen's Home uniform, explains that at the Home there is gospel singing every Friday night, plus --

Home cooked navy beans
Last year's magazines,
Makin' all your evenin's bright.

SEAMEN'S HOME COOKED NAVY BEANS

For a party of 6. Preparation time: about 1 hour and 30 minutes, after soaking.

3 cups dry navy beans
2-3 slices thick cut bacon, some excess fat removed
1 tablespoon extra virgin olive oil
1 large onion, coarsely chopped
1/2 cup chopped red bell pepper
1/2 cup chopped green bell pepper
1 teaspoon dried basil
1/2 teaspoon dried thyme
2 cups diced cooked chicken
Salt and freshly ground black pepper, to taste
Shredded mozzarella cheese

Place the beans in a large pot, cover them with water and allow to stand overnight. Drain the beans, rinse the pot, return the beans to the pot and add enough water to cover the beans. Bring to a boil over high heat. Immediately reduce the heat to simmer and cook until the beans are tender and the skins split when touched with a fork. Drain and set aside.

Cut the bacon into 1/2" pieces and fry in a large skillet over medium heat until tender-crisp. Pour or spoon any excess fat from the skillet, add the olive oil and onion and sauté until the onion is translucent. Add the red and green bell peppers and the basil and thyme and sauté for about 5 minutes. Add the chicken and beans and cook until heated through. Add salt and pepper to taste, top with the cheese and serve immediately.

♫ **THE MUSIC MAN** ♫

Book, music and lyrics by Meredith Willson
Opened December 19, 1957, at the Majestic Theatre

Born in Mason City, Iowa, in 1902, Meredith Willson said that he did not have to make up any of the innocence and heartwarming exuberance he created in River City in 1912: "All I had to do was remember." With his all-American, nostalgic story and inventively rhythmic score, including "Seventy-Six Trombones," it is ironic that Willson wrote thirty-two drafts of *The Music Man* before he could tempt a producer. And he had trouble with casting, too: Danny Kaye, Dan Dailey, Phil Harris and Gene Kelley turned down the title role of con man Harold Hill, that persuasive purveyor of dreams, that was eventually to give Robert Preston, until then known mainly as an actor in western films, his best part on Broadway.

To convince the good people of River City that "Ya Got Trouble," and, of course, that the solution is to form a marching band to combat said trouble, Harold Hill focuses his polemic on a pool table, where all the young men will spend their time:

> ". . . fritterin' away their noon-time, supper-time, chore-time, too! Get the ball in the pocket! Never mind gettin' dandelions pulled or the screen door patched or the beef steak pounded."

We'll leave it to you to determined how, if at all, you want to pound your beefsteak. Meanwhile, we'll concentrate on the townspeople who sing in anticipation of "The Wells Fargo Wagon." Consider the alliterative thoughts of one member of the chorus -- "I got some salmon from Seattle last September" -- and what might be done with that glorious fish.

71

SALMON FROM SEATTLE

For a party of 4-6. Preparation time: about 40 minutes.

1 2-pound salmon, cleaned
2 cups soft bread crumbs
1/2 teaspoon salt
1/4 cup chopped fresh Italian parsley
1/2 teaspoon poultry seasoning
1/2 teaspoon freshly grated black pepper
1/4 cup melted unsalted butter or margarine
2 tablespoons fresh lemon juice
Sliced lemons and sprigs of fresh Italian parsley, for
    garnish

Preheat the oven to 400°.   Place the salmon in a well
greased baking dish.   In a small bowl, mix the bread
crumbs, salt, chopped Italian parsley, poultry seasoning,
pepper, butter and lemon juice.   Stuff the fish with the
bread mixture and fasten the opening with a skewer or
kitchen string. Bake for about 20 minutes. Garnish with
the sliced lemons and Italian parsley sprigs and serve hot.

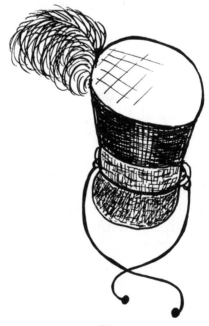

♫ PLAIN AND FANCY ♫

Book by Joseph Stein and Will Glickman
Music by Albert Hague   Lyrics by Arnold B. Horwitt
Opened January 27, 1958, at the Mark Hellinger Theatre

The title of this musical says it all.   The quiet, tradition-bound Amish community of Bird-in-Hand, Pennsylvania, is invaded by two New York sophisticates, played by Shirl Conway and Richard Derr.   In the encounter a barn is burned, and a new one communally raised, while the "plain" Amish customs are exposed. Such simplicity, however, is quickly crossed with New York naughtiness, as an Amish lad succumbs to alcohol at a carnival, and Broadway's tried and true clichés take over the plot. *Plain and Fancy* ran for 462 performances in New York and 217 at the Drury Lane Theatre in London.

The Amish are superior farmers, and food is not lacking in this musical.   In Act I, Scene 3, some of the girls, in preparation for a wedding, peel potatoes and apples, while apple butter is being churned.

AMISH APPLE BUTTER

Makes about 5 pints.   Preparation time: about 1 hour.

4 pounds flavorful cooking apples
2 cups cider vinegar
3 cups light brown sugar
2 teaspoons cinnamon
A grating of fresh nutmeg
Grated zest of 3-4 lemons

Wash, stem and quarter the apples (do not peel!).   In a large saucepan, heat the vinegar.   Add the apples and cook until very tender.   Put the fruit through a fine strainer.

73

Add the sugar, cinnamon, nutmeg and zest to the pulp. Cook over low heat, stirring frequently, until the mixture falls in sheets from a spoon, or when no liquid forms around the edge of a dollop of the butter when placed on a plate. Pour the butter into hot sterilized jars. But keep out enough to serve, warm, to your theatre party!

♬

In that same scene from Act I, local men are displaying vegetables on one of the wagons. Soon the entire cast breaks into "Plenty in Pennsylvania."

Anything grows in Pennsylvania.
Look around and you can see.
Asparagus, broccoli, cauliflower,
Dandelion greens and escarole,
Fennel and grapes and honeydew melon
And iceberg lettuce for the salad bowl.

The alphabetical list goes on, including the ingredients for the following recipe:

SQUASH AND ZUCCHINI
WITH FENNEL AND UN-I-ONS

For a party of 6.   Preparation time: about 15 minutes.

1 tablespoon unsalted butter or margarine
2 tablespoons extra virgin olive oil
1 large onion, halved and thinly sliced
1 teaspoon fennel seeds
3 medium yellow summer squash, peeled and cut in 1/4" rounds or strips
3 medium zucchini, peeled and cut in 1/4" rounds or strips
Salt and freshly ground black pepper, to taste

In a large skillet, melt the butter over medium-low heat. Add the olive oil and heat. Add the onion and sauté about 3 minutes. Add the fennel seeds, squash and zucchini, raise the heat to medium and sauté for about 5 minutes, or until the vegetables begin to brown but are still tender-crisp. Add salt and pepper to taste. Serve immediately.

Yams, it seems, also grow in Pennsylvania. A recipe appears on page 166.

It is agreed that the new bride is a great cook. Just the mention of *Kassler Ripchen und Sauerkraut* stirs the tastebuds. In Act II, Scene 1, Dan, the New Yorker, is impressed: "And did you taste this nut streusel? It's sensational. These people know how to live!" Not to mention -- how to eat!

SENSATIONAL NUT STREUSEL

For the batter:
2 cups all purpose flour
1/4 teaspoon salt
1/2 cup sugar
2 teaspoons baking powder
1 egg or 2 ounces egg substitute
1/2 cup milk
1/2 cup orange juice
1/3 cup canola or safflower oil
Grated zest of 1 orange

For the topping:
1/4 cup flour
1/2 cup sugar
1/4 cup finely chopped walnuts or pecans
3 tablespoons unsalted butter or margarine

Preheat the oven to 375°. In a large bowl, sift together the flour, salt, sugar and baking powder. Add the egg, milk, orange juice, oil and zest and stir only until the dry ingredients are dampened. Place the batter in a 9" square or round pan.

Make the topping: Mix together the flour, sugar, nuts and butter. Spread evenly on top of the batter. Bake for 30-35 minutes. Serve warm.

♫ FLOWER DRUM SONG ♫

Book and lyrics by Joseph Fields
and Oscar Hammerstein, II
Music by Richard Rodgers
Opened December 1, 1958, at the St. James Theatre

Joseph Fields was the first of the authors to be impressed with Chin Y. Lee's novel, *The Flower Drum Song*, but it was Oscar Hammerstein who, recognizing the book's strength of character and background, called it "a Chinese Life With Father." Although the theme of conflict between the Old World and the New in San Francisco's Chinatown is predictable, the acting of Miyoshi Umeki, a native Japanese playing a traditional Chinese girl, and Pat Suzuki, an American-Japanese as a Chinese-American strip-tease dancer, was met with unquestioning applause. Apparently, the cross-cultural casting did not bother the audience.

From the tone set in the popular song, *I Enjoy Being a Girl*, which shows the Americanization of a new generation of immigrants, we suspect that some of the Chinese food mentioned in *Flower Drum Song* is also Westernized. Indeed, while the soups, Ginseng and Shark-fin, are traditional Chinese dishes, Chop Suey is, for the Chinese, nothing short of an American abomination.

> Chop Suey [sings the Chorus in Act I, Scene 5],
> Chop Suey,
> Rough and tough and brittle and soft and gooey --
> Peking Duck and Mulligan stew . . .

The irony shows in the last two dishes, both traditional but, in both the preparation and the eating, springing from dramatically diverse cultures. A recipe for Mulligan stew appears on page 8, and, for those who enjoy it, here is a recipe for the rough and tough, etc.:

CHOP SUEY

For a party of 8.   Preparation time: about 30 minutes.

2 tablespoons peanut, canola or safflower oil
1 celery stalk, with leaves, cut diagonally
3 scallions, cut diagonally
1 clove garlic, minced
2 cups cooked chicken, pork or shrimp, cut into 2"
    julienne strips
1 green bell pepper, membranes and seeds removed,
    coarsely chopped
1 cup chopped fresh mushrooms
1 cup drained bean sprouts
1 cup chicken or beef stock
1 tablespoon light soy sauce
3 tablespoons Chinese rice wine or dry sherry
Salt and freshly ground white pepper, to taste
1 teaspoon cornstarch mixed with 1 teaspoon water, for
    thickening

In a wok or large skillet, heat the oil over medium-high
heat. Add the celery, scallions and garlic. Stir-fry for 3
minutes. Add the meat, bell pepper, mushrooms and
bean sprouts and stir-fry 3 minutes more. Add the stock,
soy sauce, rice wine, salt and pepper. Thicken, if
necessary, with the cornstarch. Serve over white rice (see
the instructions on page 98).

♫

And for those interested in authentic Chinese cuisine . . .

SHARK-FIN SOUP

For a party of 6-8. Preparation time: about 2 hours, after
soaking.

1/4 pound prepared shredded shark fin
2 scallions, coarsely sliced

2 1" rounds of fresh ginger, about 1/8" thick
6 cups chicken stock
1/4 pound lean pork, julienne cut
1/4 cup bamboo shoots, julienne cut
5-6 dried Chinese mushrooms, soaked and julienne cut
2 tablespoons Chinese rice wine or dry sherry
Salt, to taste
2 egg whites
Ham slivers, for garnish
Sesame oil, for garnish

Soak the shark fin overnight in cold water. Drain and place in a large saucepan, cover with fresh water and add the scallions and ginger. Bring to a boil. Immediately remove from the heat, cover and allow to cool. Drain the fin. Remove the scallions and ginger. Return the fin to the pan, add the stock, bring to a boil, reduce the heat to simmer, cover and cook for 20 minutes, or until tender. Add the pork, bamboo shoots and mushrooms and simmer for 10 minutes. Add the wine and salt. Beat the egg whites until fluffy and gently fold into the soup. Add the ham and a few drops of sesame oil. Serve immediately.

♫ GYPSY ♫

Book by Arthur Laurents   Music by Jule Styne
Lyrics by Stephen Sondheim
Opened May 21, 1959, at the Broadway Theatre

The autobiography of Gypsy Rose Lee so enchanted producer David Merrick that he secured the theatrical rights after reading only one chapter. Ethel Merman read the book and, according to rumor, was so taken with the idea of playing Rose, the quintessential Stage Mother, that she threatened to shoot anyone else who got the part. She didn't have to commit mayhem, of course, and reached a high point in her career with the raucous number at the end of Act I, "Everything's Coming Up Roses." Jack Klugman, as the sympathetic agent, Herbie, does his best to moderate the enthusiasm of the domineering, stage-struck, Rose, who must learn that if you try to live your children's lives, you'll end up destroying yourself.

Rose, however, is difficult to persuade. When Mr. Goldstone brings good news, her song says it all:

> Have an egg roll, Mr. Goldstone,
> Have a napkin, have a chopstick, have a chair!
> Have a sparerib, Mr. Goldstone --
> Any sparerib that I can spare, I'd be glad to share!
> Have a dish, have a fork,
> Have a fish, have a pork,
> Put your feet up, feel at home.

Thus, the scene is set. Have an egg roll.

ROSE'S EGG ROLLS

For a party of 8.   Preparation time: about 45 minutes.

1 tablespoon peanut, canola or safflower oil
1 1/2-pound chicken breast, skinned, boned and minced
1/2 pound shrimp, peeled, deveined and minced

1 clove garlic, minced
8 scallions, minced
1 cup chopped bean sprouts
1/2 cup finely chopped water chestnuts
1 tablespoon grated fresh ginger root
1 1/2 tablespoons light soy sauce
8 6 1/2" x 7" egg roll skins
Peanut, canola or safflower oil, for frying
Sweet and Sour sauce, for dipping

In a wok or large skillet, heat the oil over high heat. Add the chicken, shrimp, garlic and scallions and stir-fry for 3 minutes. Add the bean sprouts, water chestnuts, ginger root and soy sauce and stir-fry for a few seconds. Spread 1 tablespoon of the filling on each egg roll skin. Fold over the ends of the skin and then roll from one side to the other, tucking in the ends. Seal with a bit of water.

In the wok, heat the frying oil to 370°. Place the egg rolls in the oil and cook, turning once, until the skin is crisp, brown and bubbly. Serve with Sweet and Sour sauce.

For fish, see page 25. And for pork, see page 3.

♫

Rose and company are frequently hungry in the early scenes. Consider the following exchange in Act I, Scene 2:

Louise: That's dog food, Momma.
Rose: That's what she thinks. I'm hungry.
Louise: Then why didn't you eat some of our chow mein after the show?
Rose: Because you two did the work, and we gotta save every cent.

For Chow Mein, prepare the recipe for Chop Suey on page 78 and serve it over fried Chinese noodles.

♫ # THE SOUND OF MUSIC ♫

Book by Howard Lindsay and Russel Crouse
Music and lyrics by Richard Rodgers
and Oscar Hammerstein, II
Opened November 16, 1959, at the Lunt-Fontanne Theatre

The last musical of Rodgers and Hammerstein, *The Sound of Music* ran for more than three years in New York, starring Mary Martin as Maria and Theodore Bikel as Captain Von Trapp, and nearly twice that long in London. Although Richard Rodgers was reluctant to add new songs to the traditional music of the Trapp Family Singers, he was persuaded -- with results ranging from "Maria" to "Climb Ev'ry Mountain" and the ever-favorite "Edelweiss."

In "Do-Re-Mi" Maria teaches her young charges the rudiments of music. Ti is described as "a drink with jam and bread." Our favorite tea-time sandwich mixes generous portions of strawberry jam with marshmallow fluff on white bread to create a delight for both the eye and the palate.

Act II, Scene 11 takes place in the living room of the Trapp Villa, where people are gathered for a festive evening. As they dance to the "Laendler," Captain Von Trapp and Maria realize that they are in love. Soon, the children retire and the guests drift into the dining room -- all but Maria, who leaves for the Abbey. We aren't told what they eat at this dinner, but they might start with Austrian Old World Soup.

AUSTRIAN OLD WORLD SOUP ("MEAL IN A BOWL")

For a party of 4-6. Preparation time: about 2 hours.

2 medium onions, chopped
1 1/2 pounds pork shoulder, cubed
2 teaspoons bacon drippings or vegetable oil

1 16-ounce can sauerkraut
1 tablespoon brown sugar
1 tablespoon paprika
2 tablespoons flour
2 tablespoons tomato paste
4 beef bouillon cubes
Salt and freshly ground black pepper, to taste

In a large skillet over medium-high heat, brown the onions and pork in the bacon drippings.

Drain the sauerkraut, reserving the liquid, and add the sauerkraut to the skillet. Stir in the brown sugar, paprika, flour and tomato paste. Reduce the heat to simmer and cook for 15 minutes. Stir in the reserved liquid from the sauerkraut, the bouillon cubes and 4 cups of water. Bring just to a boil, immediately reduce the heat, cover and simmer for 50 minutes. Season with salt and pepper and serve hot.

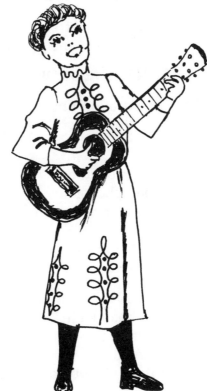

♫ LITTLE MARY SUNSHINE ♫

Book, music and lyrics by Rick Besoyan
Opened November 18, 1959, at the Orpheum Theatre

The talented author-composer-lyricist of *Little Mary Sunshine* spoofed the operettas of Rudolf Friml and Sigmund Romberg with this love story set in a Colorado Inn at the turn of the century. Eileen Brennan won an Obie as Best Actress, and the show ran for 1,143 performances. By refusing to move the somewhat wild fusion of Indians, Forest Rangers and Young Ladies from the Eastchester Finishing School to Broadway, the producers encouraged the development of the Off-Broadway musical theatre.

At the Inn, the Young Ladies and Forest Rangers enjoy "Such a Merry Party," and the Young Ladies sing:

"It's lots of fun with lots of eats -- and lots of men -- pots of dainty little sweets and pots of men --"

SUNSHINE BROWNIES

For a party of 6. Preparation time: about 45 minutes, plus cooling.

1 cup sugar
2 eggs or 4 ounces egg substitute
2 squares unsweetened chocolate
1/2 cup unsalted butter or margarine
1/2 cup flour
1 teaspoon pure vanilla extract
1/2 cup chopped walnuts

Preheat the oven to 350°. In a large bowl, combine the sugar and eggs and beat well. Melt the chocolate and butter together in a small pan and add to the egg mixture. Blend in the flour. Add the vanilla extract and walnuts. Bake for 25-35 minutes. Cool before cutting.

DAINTY LITTLE SUGAR COOKIES

Makes 6 dozen cookies.   Preparation time: 30 minutes.

1 cup vegetable shortening
1 cup plus 2 tablespoons sugar
1 egg, beaten
1 teaspoon pure vanilla extract
2 cups flour
1/2 teaspoon cream of tartar
1/2 teaspoon baking soda
1/8 teaspoon salt

Preheat the oven to 400°.   In a large bowl, cream the shortening and 1 cup sugar. Blend in the egg and vanilla. In another bowl, sift together the flour, cream of tartar, baking soda and salt. Sift this mixture into the sugar mixture and blend thoroughly. Form the dough into small balls, press each ball with the bottom of a glass that has been moistened with water and dipped in the remaining sugar. Place the cookies on an ungreased baking sheet and bake for 6-8 minutes, or until golden brown.

♬

In Act II, Scene 2, Chief Bear blesses the food to give wisdom, strength and courage to Young Billy:

Chief: Do hot do aye ah too. Do hot do aye ah too. For wisdom. Eat.
Billy: Humm. That's very tasty. Very tasty indeed.
Chief: Eagle Brain. Do hot do aye ah too. Do hot do aye ah too. For courage. Eat.
Billy: It's kind of gooey. My, oh, my, yes, Sir. What was it?
Chief: Mountain lion eyes. Do hot do aye ah too. Do hot do aye ah too. For manly strength. Eat.
Billy: I'm not very hungry. It's, it's very . . . What is it? On second thought, don't tell me.
Chief: Wash down with fire water.

EAGLE BRAIN (FOR WISDOM)

For a party of 6. Preparation time: about 1 hour, plus cooling and chilling.

1/4 cup rice
2 cups milk
1/8 teaspoon salt
1 envelope unflavored gelatin
1/3 cup sugar
1 teaspoon pure vanilla extract
1 cup whipped cream
Chocolate syrup or hot fudge, for topping

In the top of a double boiler, combine the rice, milk and salt. Cook over boiling water for 45 minutes, or until the rice is soft. Meanwhile, soak the gelatin in 1/4 cup of cold water. Add the sugar and gelatin to the rice, stirring to dissolve. Allow the mixture to cool in the refrigerator. When the gelatin begins to set, add the vanilla extract. Fold in the whipped cream. Pour the mixture into a mold and chill. Serve topped with chocolate syrup or hot fudge.

MOUNTAIN LION EYES (FOR COURAGE)

For a party of 6-8. Preparation time: about 15 minutes.

1 box vanilla wafers, finely crushed
3/4 cup grated coconut
3/4 cup confectioners sugar
1/3 cup undiluted frozen orange juice

In a large bowl, mix the ingredients together. Form into walnut-sized balls and serve. Do hot do aye ah too.

♫ FIORELLO! ♫

Book by Jerome Weidman and George Abbott
Music by Jerry Bock   Lyrics by Sheldon Harnick
Opened November 23, 1959, at the Broadhurst Theatre

The great challenge for the producers of this biographical musical was to cast the right actor as the "Little Flower." After testing about two hundred hopefuls -- from Mickey Rooney to Eli Wallach -- they chose Tom Bosley, a complete unknown on Broadway, who brought all they could desire to the many-sided character they had created. Bosley had only one major song -- "The Name's La Guardia" -- to embellish his portrayal, but critic Henry Hewes thought the actor captured more of "La Guardia's essence than the man did himself when he was alive." In spite of an Actor's Equity strike that closed thirteen musicals, *Fiorello!* ran for 796 perforances and gathered a bouquet of awards including the Pulitzer Prize, the New York Drama Critics Circle Award and, shared with *The Sound of Music*, the Tony for Best Musical of the Season.

With a hero who was half-Italian, half-Jewish, and a bonafide native of New York -- where eating out is a popular recreation -- *Fiorello!* might lead one to expect a spicy pasta dish, a succulent Kosher chicken or a sidewalk vendor's salty pretzel. Alas, the only food mentioned is a simple roast. In Act I, Scene 1, Morris, the manager of La Guardia's office in Greenwich Village, speaks to his wife on the phone:

> Shirley, how can I tell you when to put the roast in? No, Shirley, only God and Mr. La Guardia know when I'll be there, and neither one tells me till the last minute.

Again in Act II, Scene 5, the roast is mentioned during a touching scene in which La Guardia, after an assassination attempt, castigates Morris and a young law clerk named

Neil for shirking their responsibilities when they are, in fact, trying to break the news that Mrs. La Guardia has died suddenly.

What a team! Any of your dikes spring a leak lately? Send for Neil and Morris, and watch your whole damn country get flooded away before the night's over! . . . (to Morris) Did you have anybody on that roof? Or were you just too damn busy on the phone telling Shirley when to put the roast in?

Never mind. This roast is good!

NEW YORK CITY ROAST BEEF

For a party of 4-6. Preparation time: about 3 hours and 30 minutes.

3 tablespoons extra virgin olive oil
1 3-pound chuck roast
1/8 teaspoon (or less) salt
1 teaspoon freshly ground black pepper
12 small new potatoes in their jackets
3-4 carrots, scraped and cut into 2" pieces
12 small (1 1/2" - 2") white onions, peeled
2 large garlic cloves, peeled and coarsely chopped
1/2 teaspoon dried oregano
1 teaspoon dried basil
1 teaspoon chili powder
2 teaspoons Worcestershire sauce
1 small red onion, coarsely chopped
12 large mushrooms, trimmed and quartered

Preheat the oven to 325°. Heat a large skillet over medium heat and add the oil. When the oil is hot, add the roast and cook, turning frequently, until evenly browned on all sides. Sprinkle the roast with salt and pepper and place on a rack in a roasting pan. Arrange the potatoes, carrots and white onions around the roast.

Combine a cup of water with the garlic, oregano, basil, chili powder, Worcestershire sauce and red onion and place in a blender. Blend until smooth. Pour the sauce over the meat and vegetables. Bake for about 2 1/2 hours, basting frequently with the sauce.

Place the mushrooms around and on top of the roast. Bake for 30 minutes more, basting once or twice. Remove the roast from the pan. Place the vegetables in a serving dish and keep warm. Allow the roast to stand for 15 minutes before carving.

♫ CARNIVAL ♫

Book by Michael Stewart
Music and lyrics by Bob Merrill
Opened April 13, 1961, at the Imperial Theatre

The *New York Times* called this Broadway version of the film, *Lili*, "sentiment and show business razzle-dazzle" turned into "flashy, eye-filling and occasionally touching entertainment." With *Carnival*, which starred Anna Mara Alberghetti as Lili, Gower Champion became one of the foremost directors of musical theatre.

At a carnival, people are always hungry, performers and wandering viewers alike. At the Puppet Booth in Act I, Scene 2, Marco the Magnificent describes to Lili the kind of person he wants to take to dinner: "Someone who'll appreciate a bit of cheese . . . a glass of wine . . . some cold chicken." If you, too, appreciate these things, prepare Southern Hospitality Chicken (page 6) and refrigerate it for several hours or overnight. Serve the chicken with cool white wine and Brie on French bread.

♫

Later in the Main Tent (Act 1, Scene 6) Lili is amazed as Marco pulls food from a volunteer's pocket.

> He found sausages and sausages.
> I never, I just never have seen
> Anything as clever in my life!
> First he took out a brioche,
> Then a sausage . . .

MARCO'S SAUSAGES, IN BLANKETS

For a party of 6. Preparation time: about 40 minutes.

1 1/2 cups flour
1/4 teaspoon salt

3 teaspoons baking powder
3 tablespoons vegetable shortening
1/2 cup plus 2 tablespoons milk
6 pork sausages
Dijon or honey mustard

Preheat the oven to 400 degrees F. In a large bowl sift together, twice, the flour, salt and baking power. Cut in the shortening and stir in the milk. On a well-floured surface, roll out the dough into a rectangle 1/4" thick. Cut the dough into 6 squares.

In a large skillet over medium-high heat, cook the sausages until about half done. Drain well on several folds of paper toweling. Roll each sausage in a square of dough, leaving the ends open. Bake on a well greased baking sheet for about 15 minutes. Serve hot, with the mustard as a dip.

♫

In Act I, Scene 7, at the Puppet Booth, Lili talks to the puppets, who respond in a happy song with cheerful words such as fish, peaches on shortcake, clams and tuna fish. Love, as the song says, "makes the world go round," but good food helps it along, too!

PEACH SHORTCAKE

For a party of 4-6. Preparation time: about 30 minutes, including baking.

2/3 cup milk
1 egg
2 cups unbleached flour
1/4 teaspoon salt
1/3 cup sugar
4 teaspoons baking powder

2 tablespoons vegetable shortening
Unsalted butter or margarine
2-3 fresh peaches, peeled and cubed or thinly sliced, chilled
Whipped cream, for topping

Preheat the oven to 425°.   In a small bowl, mix the milk
and egg. In a large bowl, combine the flour, salt, sugar and
baking powder.   Cut in the shortening. Stir the milk and
egg mixture into the flour mixture to make a soft dough.
Spread the dough in well-greased cake pan. Bake for 12-15
minutes.

While the cake is still warm, remove it from the pan, split
it horizontally and spread the bottom layer with the
butter.   Arrange 1/2 of the peaches on the bottom layer,
top with the other layer and with the remaining peaches.
Serve warm, topped with the whipped cream.

CARNIVAL CLAMS

For a party of 4-6.   Preparation time: about 20 minutes.

Canola or safflower oil, for deep frying
3 cups flour
1/2 teaspoon salt
3 teaspoons baking powder
3 eggs, well beaten, or 6 ounces egg substitute
2 1/4 - 3 cups milk
3 dozen medium-sized clams

Place the oil in a deep fryer and heat to 375°.   In a large
bowl, sift together the flour, salt and baking powder. Stir
in the eggs and enough milk to make a thin batter. Dip
the clams into the batter. Deep fry until golden brown.
Serve hot.

♬ BYE BYE BIRDIE ♬

Book by Michael Stewart   Music by Charles Strouse
Lyrics by Lee Adams
Opened April 14, 1960, at the Martin Beck Theatre

Faced with satirizing a kind of music -- rock and roll --
that was itself very new, the writers created Conrad Birdie,
played by Dick Gautier and modeled on Elvis Presley, and
burlesqued the singing idol and his much-publicized
induction into the army. Songs like "One Last Kiss," "One
Boy" and "A Lot of Living to Do" appealed to high
schoolers, as did the story line. Trying to avoid disaster
for their Almaelou Music Corporation, Albert Peterson,
played by Dick Van Dyke, and his secretary Rose, played by
Chita Rivera, arrange for Birdie to "kiss goodbye" Kim
MacAfee, age 15, president of the Conrad Birdie Fan Club
#2748.

In Act II, Scene 7, Albert manages to think of something
besides Birdie and proposes to Rose, who answers in song:

I'm just a Spanish tamale
I'll be so Spanish it will make you sick!
I'll eat the tacos and the enchiladas!
I'll drink tequila till I feel-a no pain!

Our suggestion: savor the enchiladas and go easy on the
tequila.

ROSE'S ENCHILADAS

For a party of 6.   Preparation time: about 1 hour.

6 ounces chorizo sausage, casings removed, crumbled
1 1-pound can refried beans, or Frijoles Refritas (page 190)
1 tablespoon extra virgin olive oil

93

1 medium onion, finely chopped
1-2 cloves garlic, minced
1 15-ounce can tomato sauce
2 cans green chili peppers, chopped
1 teaspoon chili powder
1 teaspoon ground cumin
12 corn tortillas
1 cup shredded cheddar cheese
1 cup shredded jack cheese
2-3 scallions, chopped, for garnish

Preheat the oven to 375°. In a large skillet over medium heat, sauté the chorizo until browned. Drain on paper towels. Remove and discard the drippings from the skillet and return the chorizo to the skillet. Stir in the beans and cook, stirring frequently, until heated through. Remove from the heat and set aside.

Heat the oil in a small skillet over medium heat, add the onion and sauté until translucent. Add the garlic and sauté for about 4-5 minutes. Stir in 3/4 of the tomato sauce, 1/4 cup of water, the green chilis, chili powder and cumin. Raise the heat to high, bring to a boil, immediately reduce the heat to simmer and cook for 10 minutes. Dip the tortillas, one at a time, into the hot mixture until limp. Fill each tortilla with about 3 tablespoons of the bean mixture. Spread about 2 tablespoons of the remaining tomato sauce in the bottom of a baking dish. Roll the tortillas and arrange them, seam side down, in the dish. Top with the remaining tomato sauce and sprinkle with the cheeses. Bake for about 30 minutes, sprinkle with the scallions and serve immediately.

For a recipe for tacos, see page 189.

♫ THE FANTASTICKS ♫

Book and lyrics by Tom Jones   Music by Harvey Schmidt
Opened May 3, 1960, at the Sullivan Street Playhouse

After more than thirty years and 14,000 performances, *The Fantasticks* is far and away America's longest running musical. With a commedia dell'arte approach and a plot based on Edmund Rostand's *Les Romanesques, The Fantasticks* is a simple love story from a time when "life was young and, oh, so tender." Knowing that love without obstacles tends to wither, the fathers of the young lovers arrange for a troubadour, El Gallo, originally played by Jerry Orbach, to bring tension to their lives, only to discover that the moonlight romance of Act I requires the sunlit reality of Act II for love to mature.

"Try to Remember" may be the most enduring song in this show, but "Plant a Radish" presents a metaphor for a society obsessed with childcare, as the two fathers compare raising children and cultivating vegetables.

> Plant a radish,
> Get a radish.
> Never any doubt
> That's why I love vegetables;
> You know what you're about!

But with children there is less certainty, as the fathers discover:

> It's bewilderin'
> You don't know until the seed is nearly grown
> Just what you've sown.
> So
> Plant a carrot,
> Get a carrot,

Not a brussel sprout.
That's why I love vegetables
You know what you're about!

And with knowledge come happiness and pleasure. On this point the fathers agree. The following recipe doesn't include carrots, radishes or sprouts, but most of the ingredients can be found in the garden, and the results are certain!

FANTASTICK VEGETABLE CASSEROLE

For a party of 6.   Preparation time: about 1 hour.

1 large white onion, peeled and thinly sliced
2 large cloves garlic, finely minced
2 tablespoons fresh lemon thyme leaves
2-3 bay leaves, finely crumbled
1 medium eggplant, thinly sliced
1-2 zucchini, peeled and thinly sliced
1-2 ripe tomatoes, thinly sliced
Salt and freshly ground black pepper, to taste
Extra virgin olive oil

Preheat the oven to 350°. Arrange a layer of onion slices in a large flat baking dish that has been sprayed with non-stick spray. Sprinkle with 1/4 each of the garlic, thyme leaves and bay leaves. Arrange a layer of eggplant slices on top of the onion, and repeat the process with the garlic, thyme and bay leaves. Repeat the process with the zucchini and tomato slices. Sprinkle with salt and pepper. Generously drizzle olive oil over the top of the casserole and bake, uncovered, for 30 minutes. Cover loosely with foil and bake for 15-20 minutes more. Serve hot.

♫ TENDERLOIN ♫

Book by Jerome Weidman and George Abbott
Music by Jerry Bock   Lyrics by Sheldon Harnick
Opened October 17, 1960, at the Forty-Sixth Street Theatre

The Tenderloin district of Manhattan -- New York's busiest red light district during the 1890's -- stretched from 14th Street to 42nd Street and from Fourth Avenue to the Hudson River. As the land of opportunity for prostitutes, corrupt police and sleazy reporters, it seems an excellent place for the Reverend Brock (originated by Maurice Evans in his first singing role in nearly thirty years) to work his moralizing magic. His adversary, Tommy (Ron Husmann), is a reporter who sings in a bordello for extra cash. Surprisingly, Bock and Harnick's songs, such as "Artificial Flowers," "The Picture of Happiness" and "Good Clean Fun," seem to give the people of the Tenderloin the edge in the fight. The show had a run of twenty-seven weeks.

Clark's is a popular Tenderloin haunt. As Lieutenant Schmidt of the police tells the Reverend Brock: "Sin is what makes this town go round. People want it. It's what keeps both you and me in business." Clark's is also the place of Tommy's musical employment. Tommy and Maggie, a prostitute, sing:

> He fed (he fed)
> Her lobster (her lobster)
> And sparkling wine (and sparkling wine)
> That crafty old swine (that crafty old swine) . . .

At least, he fed her lobster -- as "her head began to swim" and "he gratified his whim."

One may also gratify a whim -- for lobster.

LOBSTER TENDERLOIN

For a party of 6.   Preparation time: about 1 hour and 30 minutes.

2 cups white rice
2 1 1/4-pound lobsters
2 tablespoons extra virgin olive oil
1 large onion, peeled and chopped
2 cloves garlic, peeled and minced
1/2 cup thinly sliced red bell pepper
2 tablespoons flour
1/2 cup half-and-half
1/2 cup (or more) milk
2 teaspoons ground cumin
1 tablespoon chopped pickled jalapeño pepper
1/4 cup Dijon mustard
1/2 cup shredded Swiss cheese

In a large saucepan with a tightly fitting lid, bring the rice and 4 cups of cold water to a boil. Cover, reduce the heat to simmer and cook for 15 minutes. Remove from the heat and let stand for 5 minutes.

Meanwhile, in a large pot with a tightly fitting lid, bring about 2" of water to a full boil over high heat. Add the lobsters, head first, and immediately cover the pot and reduce the heat to low. Cook the lobsters for about 13 minutes, or until they turn an even, bright red color. Remove from the pot and allow to cool. As soon as the lobsters are cool enough to handle, remove the meat from the claws, tail and any other sections you care to tackle. Reserve any roe (reddish in color) or tomalley (greenish). Cut the meat into bite-sized chunks.

Heat the oil in a large skillet over medium heat and add the onion. Sauté for 10 minutes. Add the garlic and bell pepper and sauté for 5 minutes more. Add the lobster meat and flour and gently sauté until the flour just begins to brown. Add the half-and-half, 1/2 cup of milk, cumin, jalapeño and mustard. Cook, stirring constantly, until the sauce thickens, adding a bit more milk if the sauce becomes too thick. Gently fold in the roe and/or tomalley.

Place the rice on a warm serving platter and top with the lobster and sauce. Sprinkle with the cheese and serve immediately with sparkling white wine.

♫ CAMELOT ♫

Book and lyrics by Frederick Loewe
Music by Alan J. Lerner
Opened December 3, 1960, at the Majestic Theatre

For many Americans, the title song of *Camelot* is still nostalgically associated with the Kennedy administration. On a sad note, it was the last show for the team of Lerner and Loewe, whose temperamental differences precluded further collaboration. With a spectacular cast -- Richard Burton as Arthur, Julie Andrews as Guenevere, Robert Goulet as Lancelot, Roddy McDowell as Mordred -- *Camelot* seemed a sure hit, but it faltered immediately. Not until director Moss Hart, hospitalized by a heart attack, and Lerner, laid up with bleeding ulcers, could return for a serious revision, did the musical succeed, running for 873 performances. In a revival at the Gershwin Theatre in 1993, Robert Goulet again starred -- this time as King Arthur!

In Act II, Scene 4, it becomes clear that Morgan Le Fey loves to eat and, in particular, she loves to eat candy.

> Morgan Le Fey: My chairs are made of vegetables; my table's made of cheese, and my doors are gingerbread. . . . Roast beef, wall to wall. But candy, I never get, so I desire it most of all.

MORGAN LE FEY'S GINGERBREAD

For a party of 8-10. Preparation time: about 1 hour.

6 whole cloves
1/2 cup unsalted butter or margarine
1/2 cup sugar
1 egg or 2 ounces egg substitute

1 cup dark molasses
2 1/4 cups sifted flour
1 teaspoon baking soda
1/4 teaspoon salt
1 teaspoon ginger
1 teaspoon cinnamon

Bring 1 cup of water to a boil in a small pan. Add the cloves and boil for about 2 minutes. Remove and discard the cloves. Set the water aside.

Preheat the oven to 325°. In a large bowl, cream the butter and sugar. Add the egg and mix thoroughly. Add the reserved water, the egg and the molasses and blend thoroughly. In another bowl, sift together the flour, baking soda, salt, ginger and cinnamon and add to the butter mixture. Stir to mix thoroughly. Pour the batter into a well greased and floured 9" square pan. Bake for 45-50 minutes. Serve warm, with applesauce (see page 115) or sweetened whipped cream.

♬

Mordred, of course, is not above taking advantage of an idiosyncrasy which many of us share.

> Mordred: Masses and masses
>   Of gummy molasses,
>   Fudge by the van!
>   Fresh marzipan!

MORDRED'S MOLASSES FUDGE

For a party of 8-10. Preparation time: about 40 minutes, plus cooling.

2 cups sugar
1/8 teaspoon salt

2 teaspoons molasses
5 teaspoons (or more) cocoa
1 cup milk
1/2 teaspoon pure vanilla extract

Combine all the ingredients in a saucepan and cook over low heat until the mixture reaches 234° on a candy thermometer and forms a soft ball in cold water. Remove from the heat and beat until cool and thick. Pour into a buttered dish and allow to cool completely before cutting.

For recipes for roast beef, see pages 88 and 169. For cheese, see page 171. And for vegetables, see the Index to Recipes.

♫ A FUNNY THING ♫
HAPPENED
ON THE WAY TO THE FORUM

Book by Burt Shevelove and Larry Gelbart
Music and lyrics by Stephen Sondheim
Opened May 8, 1962, at the Alvin Theatre

The authors were quick to confess that all the jokes in their musical, as well as all the comic characters and farcical situations, first appeared in the plays of Plautus, a prolific Roman dramatist who died about 184 B.C. but whose work still survives, mainly on college stages. The resulting adaptation, *A Funny Thing Happened on the Way to the Forum*, is a marathon of bawdy slapstick comedy and farce that Abbott, as director, whipped along at breakneck speed with a cast including Zero Mostel as Pseudolus (a role originally intended for Milton Berle), Jack Gilford, David Burns and John Carradine. Sondheim admitted that the music mainly allowed people a respite from laughing, but it also helped to establish the mood: "Pretty Little Picture," "Everybody Ought to Have a Maid," and "Bring Me My Bride." The show won a Tony Award for Best Musical and had a successful London production and a Tony-winning revival in 1972, with Phil Silvers.

The opening musical number explains everything: "Comedy Tonight!" When Senex and his wife prepare to leave the city, Hysterium (Jack Gilford), a slave, has been ordered to keep Hero, their son, innocent of the pleasures that Hero's slave, Pseudolus, finds most attractive. An appetite for food is, obviously, not the appetite of major concern in the play, but it is mentioned in Act II, as people appear in Senex's house: "There is food and drink within." No details are provided, but we suggest a dish of Farfalle and Olives.

FARFALLE AND OLIVES

For a party of 4-6.   Preparation time: about 20 minutes.

1 pound farfalle (bowtie pasta)
1/2 cup extra virgin olive oil
1/2 cup finely chopped ripe olives, well drained
1/2 cup finely chopped stuffed salad olives, well drained
203 tablespoons capers, well drained
4-5 cloves garlic, finely minced
Freshly grated Romano cheese

Cook the farfalle *al dente* according to package directions.
While the pasta cooks, heat the oil in a large skillet over
medium heat. Add the olives and capers and sauté for 5
minutes.   Add the garlic and sauté until just golden.
When the pasta is done, drain and add to the olive
mixture, tossing to mix evenly and coat the pasta with oil.
Top with the cheese and serve immediately with crusty
Italian bread.

♫ HELLO, DOLLY! ♫

Book by Michael Stewart
Music and lyrics by Jerry Herman
Opened January 1, 1964, at the St. James Theatre

One almost automatically thinks of Carol Channing as Dolly Levi in the musical adaptation of Thornton Wilder's *The Matchmaker* (1954), but a number of movie stars stepped into her Broadway shoes when she took the show on tour: Ginger Rogers, Martha Raye and Betty Grable. Ethel Merman, for whom the musical was originally written, was the final Dolly when the show closed in 1970, after 2,844 performances. Dorothy Lamour headed the cast of a touring version, and in 1967 Pearl Bailey played Dolly in New York with an all-black cast. After winning Drama Critics Circle and Tony Awards for Best Musical, *Hello, Dolly!* was also a hit in London, with Mary Martin in the title role.

Dolly is described as "a woman who arranges things -- the furniture, daffodils and lives." In Act II, at the Harmonia Gardens Restaurant at "eight o'clock tonight," there is to be a chicken dinner. Dolly will be there -- to arrange things. You come, too.

CHICKEN FOR EIGHT AT EIGHT

For a party of 8. Preparation time: about 1 hour and 15 minutes.

1 tablespoon canola or safflower oil
2 fryers, cut into serving pieces
1 lemon, cut in half
Salt and freshly ground black pepper, to taste
1/2 cup dry white wine
3 tablespoons brandy
1 medium onion, minced
1-2 cloves garlic, minced

In a large skillet, heat the oil. Rub the chicken with the lemon and season with salt and pepper. Brown the chicken on all sides in the oil. Remove from the skillet and keep warm.

Add the wine and brandy to the skillet and raise the heat to bring the sauce to a boil. Set aflame, shaking the skillet until the flame dies.

Return the chicken to the skillet, add the onion and garlic, reduce the heat to simmer, cover and cook for 45-50 minutes. If necessary, add a little water during cooking. Remove the chicken to a warm serving dish. Season the sauce to taste with salt and freshly ground black pepper, pour over the chicken and serve immediately.

♫ FUNNY GIRL ♫

Book by Isobel Lennart   Music by Jule Styne
Lyrics by Bob Merrill
Opened March 26, 1964, at the Winter Garden Theatre

Before it opened on Broadway, *Funny Girl* had a number of titles (*A Very Special Person, My Man, The Luckiest People*), several announced or rumored leading ladies (Mary Martin, Anne Bancroft, Carol Burnett), four changes of directors, innumerable rewrites (including forty revisions of the first scene) and five postponements of the premiere. But it all seemed worthwhile when twenty-one year old Barbra Streisand -- described by one critic as "more gnu than gazelle" -- finally starred in the role of Fanny Brice, whose life and career the musical portrayed. The message was "I'm the Greatest Star," but other songs such as "People" and "Don't Rain on My Parade" have remained more popular.

Act I, Scene 13, takes place in a private dining room in Baltimore. Fanny's future husband Nick, played by Sydney Chaplin, is ordering:

Nick: Paté Strasbourg, I think. Then a filet de boeuf, sauce bordelaise. Pommes de terre soufflé, endive, and stemmed strawberries. A very light Bordeaux with the filet de boeuf --
Waiter: Saint Emilion -- 1905?
Nick: Perfect.
Fanny (sings): Just some dried-out toast in a sliver,
On the top a little chopped liver.
(Hide the paté)
How many girls become a sinner
While waiting for a roast beef dinner?

The question might be posed: Is dinner worth sinning for? We think it might be, if the sin is just a little one, and the dinner is as follows.

We recommend that you begin with paté (see page 186), as Nick suggests; then, present our menu, followed by a simple endive salad and, finally, fresh strawberries.

FILET DE BOEUF

For a party of 12-15.   Preparation time: about 40 minutes.

2-3 tablespoons unsalted butter
A 5-pound fillet or tenderloin of beef, fat and sinew
    removed
Salt and freshly ground black pepper, to taste.

Preheat the oven to 500°.   Rub the butter generously over the fillet. Fold over the thin end of the fillet and tie it in place with kitchen string. Place the fillet on a rack in a well greased roasting pan and place in the oven. Immediately reduce the heat to 400° and bake for about 30 minutes. (When your meat thermometer reads 130°, the meat is cooked rare.) Season the fillet with salt and pepper and serve immediately.

SAUCE BORDELAISE

For a party of 12-15.   Preparation time: about 2 hours, including simmering.

A 4" beef marrow bone
2 sprigs fresh parsley
1/4 teaspoon dried thyme
1 bay leaf
6-8 whole black peppercorns
2 1/2 tablespoons unsalted butter or margarine
1/3 cup finely chopped onion
1/3 cup finely chopped carrot
1/3 cup finely chopped celery
3 tablespoons unbleached flour
1 3/4 cups hot beef stock
2/3 cup dry white wine

1 1/2 tablespoons tomato paste
4-5 black peppercorns, crushed
1/2 cup dry red wine
1/2 teaspoon chopped parsley

Stand the marrow bone on end and split it with a cleaver and carefully remove the marrow. (If you don't have a cleaver, ask your butcher to remove the marrow.) With a very sharp small knife dipped in water, slice the marrow into 1/4" slices. Rinse the marrow gently under cold running water. In a small saucepan, bring water to a boil over high heat. Drop in the marrow. Immediately remove from the heat and let stand until the marrow has softened, about 2 minutes. Drain and set aside.

Tie the parsley, thyme, bay leaf and peppercorns in cheesecloth to make a bouquet garni. Heat a medium saucepan over moderately low heat. Add the butter and melt. Add the onion, carrot and celery and sauté until softened but not brown, about 10 minutes. Remove from heat and add the flour, blending until the vegetables are evenly coated. Return the pan to the heat and cook, stirring frequently, until the flour is golden brown, about 10 minutes. Add the stock, white wine and tomato paste, stirring constantly until blended. Add the bouquet garni. Raise the heat to high and bring to a boil. Immediately reduce the heat to simmer and cook, stirring occasionally, until the mixture is reduced by half, about 40 minutes.

While the sauce simmers, mix the crushed peppercorns into the red wine and cook in a small saucepan over moderately low heat until reduced by 3/4.

Strain the sauce and discard the vegetables and the bouquet garni. Add the red wine mixture to the sauce and simmer for 15 minutes. Gently fold in the marrow and chopped parsley.

POMMES DE TERRE SOUFLÉ

For a party of 12-15.   Preparation time: about 1 hour.

8-10 large, very mature potatoes
Vegetable oil, for deep frying
Salt, to taste

Cut each potato into the largest possible brick shape. Slice each brick into uniform rectangles 1/8" thick. Slice off the corners of each rectangle to produce the traditional polygon. Place the slices in ice water and let soak for 25 minutes or more. Dry the slices completely.

Fill a deep fryer with oil to 1/3 capacity. Heat the oil to 275°. Drop the potato slices, one at a time, into the oil. Do not crowd the slices! The slices will sink and then, after a few seconds, rise. Very carefully (to keep from getting a burn!) shake the deep fryer to create a continuous flowing motion. Cook the potatoes, turning at least once, until the centers begin to clarify and the texture of the cut edges changes. Remove the potatoes from the deep fryer and drain for about 5 minutes. (At this point, the potatoes may be refrigerated -- and then returned to room temperature -- before the second cooking.) Add enough oil to fill the deep fryer to 1/3 capacity. Raise the heat of the oil to 385°. Return the potatoes, one at a time, to the deep fryer and -- again very carefully -- agitate the pan until the potatoes puff. Cook until the potatoes are golden brown, drain and dry on several thicknesses of paper toweling. Season with salt and serve in a basket.

Note: You might give any duds (and do expect a few!) a second chance to puff by allowing them to cool and then returning them to the deep fryer.

♫ FIDDLER ON THE ROOF ♫

Book by Joseph Stein   Music by Jerry Bock
Lyrics by Sheldon Harnick
Opened September 22, 1964, at the Imperial Theatre

"This is not just a show about Jews living in Russia in 1905, although it is that, on the surface. At its heart it's about the enduring strength of the human spirit -- and man's ability to grow, to change to overcome adversity." With these words Richard Altman, author of *The Making of a Musical, Fiddler on the Roof*, spoke to rehearsing actors in Tel Aviv, Amsterdam, London and Paris. This is, particularly, the story of Sholom Aleichem's optimistic milkman, Tevye, who struggles valiantly to keep his family together under ever changing conditions. Zero Mostel was unforgettable in the role, especially in his spirited singing of "If I Were a Rich Man." In the original production Maria Karnilova portrayed Tevye's wife and Beatrice Arthur created a sensation as Yente the Matchmaker. The show ran for 3,242 performances in New York and for 2,030 performances at Her Majesty's Theatre in London.

There is a great deal of food in *Fiddler on the Roof*: fresh fish is hawked; Tevye's daughters peel potatoes; Lazar Wolf, the rejected suitor, gives a wedding gift of five chickens. In Act I, Scene 2, Tevye offers cheese to Perchik, a student who will teach his five daughters in exchange for food. "Good," says Tevye, "Stay with us for the Sabbath. Of course, we don't eat like kings, but we don't starve, either. As the Good Book says, 'When a poor man eats a chicken, one of them is sick.'" And, in Scene 8, as the villagers pass by Motel's tailor shop, a man is selling "Bagels, fresh bagels." The audience is sure to leave the theatre with a hearty appetite!

FRESH BAGELS

Makes 18 bagels. Preparation time: about 2 hours, plus chilling.

1 cup scalded milk
1/4 cup unsalted butter or margarine
2 tablespoons sugar
1/2 teaspoon salt
1 package active dry yeast
2 eggs
3 3/4 cups (or more) sifted flour
1 egg white

Combine the scalded milk, butter, 1 tablespoon sugar and the salt in a large bowl. When the mixture cools to 105°-115°, add the yeast and dissolve for 3 minutes. Add the eggs and flour and blend well to form a soft dough. Knead the dough for 10 minutes, adding more flour if necessary. Place the dough in a greased bowl, cover and let rise in a warm place until doubled in bulk. Punch down the dough and divide into 18 equal portions. Roll each portion into a 7" rope, tapering at the ends. Moisten and seal the ends to form rings. Place the rings on a floured board, cover and let rise for 15 minutes. Chill the rings for about 2 hours.

Preheat the oven to 400°. Bring 2 quarts of water almost to a boil in a large pot, add the remaining sugar and drop in the bagels, one at a time. When they rise to the surface, turn them over and continue cooking for 3 minutes. With a large slotted spoon, remove the bagels from the water, place them on an ungreased baking sheet. Beat the egg white and brush over the bagels. Bake for 20-25 minutes, or until golden. Serve with cream cheese and lox or smoked salmon.

♫ MAN OF LA MANCHA ♫

Book by Dale Wasserman   Music by Mitch Leigh
Lyrics by Joe Darion
Opened November 22, 1965,
at the ANTA Washington Square Theatre

Impressed with the thought of the Spanish writer Miguel de Unamuno that "only he who attempts the ridiculous may achieve the impossible," Wasserman turned a teleplay based on Miguel de Cervantes' masterpiece into one of the most theatrically innovative productions of the musical stage. Richard Kiley, playing the Don, was supported by Irving Jacobson as Sancho and Joan Diener as Aldonza. Even deprived of a comforting intermission, audiences were enchanted by "The Impossible Dream," a huge hit which impelled people onward: "My destiny calls and I go."

"To Each His Dulcinea," sings Don Quixote; "To every man his dream," but Aldonza/Dulcinea gets a bit upset with both his dream and her world. At one point she approaches the Muleteers with a pot of stew in her hands.

> Aldonza (roughly): You want it on the table or over your lousy heads?
> (The Muleteers laugh. She sets down the tureen with a crash, and spits into it.)
> There, swine. Feed!

Well . . . we don't endorse the service, but the stew -- minus one ingredient -- has possibilities.

ALDONZA'S STEW

For a party of 6-8. Preparation time: about 2 hours and 30 minutes.

2 tablespoons (or more) extra virgin olive oil
1 large onion, chopped

1 green bell pepper, membranes and seeds removed, chopped
2 cloves garlic, chopped
1 fryer, skin and bones removed, cut into 1 1/2" chunks
1 28-ounce can whole peeled tomatoes, cut into 1" chunks, and their liquid
1 small can chopped green chili peppers
1/8 teaspoon (or more, or less) ground red pepper flakes
1 teaspoon ground cumin
1 bay leaf
1 large potato, cut into 1" chunks
1/2 cup frozen peas
1/2 cup frozen corn

Heat the oil in a large skillet over medium heat. Add the onion and sauté for about 10 minutes. Add the bell pepper, garlic and chicken and sauté until the chicken is lightly browned on all sides, adding more oil as needed.

Add the tomatoes, green chili peppers, ground red pepper, cumin and bay leaf. Reduce the heat to simmer, cover and cook for 1 hour. Add the potato and simmer for about 30 minutes. Add the peas and corn and simmer for 15 minutes more. Remove the bay leaf. Serve immediately in a warm tureen.

♫ MAME ♫

Book by Jerome Lawrence and Robert E. Lee
Music and lyrics by Jerry Herman
Opened May 24, 1966, at the Winter Garden Theatre

"Live! Life is a banquet and most poor sons-of-bitches are starving to death." (Act II, Scene 4)

Building upon Patrick Dennis' novel, *Auntie Mame*, about an orphaned boy whose life is taken over by his madcap aunt, and upon the dramatization by Lawrence and Lee, *Mame* had 1,508 performances with Angela Lansbury in the title role and Beatrice Arthur as her bosom friend. In the London production in 1969, Ginger Rogers played Mame. Jerry Herman said that, rather than simply a songwriter, he wanted to be a composer-lyricist for the American musical theatre -- a musical playwright. With *Mame*, he came close to achieving that goal.

One of the many comical scenes occurs in Act I, Scene 10, as Mame, a Northerner, meets her soon-to-be mother-in-law, a Southerner.

> Mother Burnside (to Beau, her son and Mame's husband-to-be): When we got peaches right here, ripe for the pickin', I cain't see why any man would go hankerin' after some Northern alligator pears.
> Beau: Mother, the War between the States is over.
> Mother Burnside (dismissing such nonsense): Don't give me any of that Appomattox Applesauce.

We dedicate our recipe to Mame.

APPOMATTOX APPLESAUCE

For a party of 8. Preparation time: about 30 minutes, plus chilling.

8 golden delicious apples, peeled, cored and sliced
1 teaspoon fresh lemon juice

1/2 cup (or more) sugar
1-2 teaspoons cinnamon
1/8 teaspoon nutmeg

Place the apples, lemon juice and 1/2 cup of water in a saucepan, cover tightly and cook over moderate heat for about 15 minutes. Stir in the sugar and cook for 5 minutes. Remove from the heat and beat to form a smooth sauce. Stir in the cinnamon and nutmeg. Serve well chilled.

♫

Before beating a retreat from Mother Burnside's South, Mame is serenaded by some boys who view her in a supposedly more kindly light:

> Well, shut my mouth
> And freeze my face,
> You've brought some elegance to this place.
> There's sourbelly, hominy, catfish and tripe, Mame!

We don't attempt to sell you on sourbelly or tripe, but you can find hominy grits on page 123 and fried fish on page 25.

♫ CABARET ♫

Book by Joe Masteroff   Music by John Kander
Lyrics by Fred Ebb
Opened November 20, 1966, at the Broadhurst Theatre

"A city called Berlin in a country called Germany -- and it was the end of the world and I was dancing with Sally Bowles -- and we were both fast asleep . . . ." (Act II, Scene 7) These are the final thoughts of an American novelist (played by Bert Convy) as he says "Goodbye" to Sally (Jill Hayworth), a singer at the Kit Kat Klub and a personification of the aimless decadence that permeated Germany just before the rise of the Third Reich. One of the early "concept" musicals, *Cabaret* gathers its theme from Christopher Isherwood's *Berlin Stories* and John Van Druten's *I Am a Camera.* Lotte Lenya as Fraulein Schneider and Jack Gilford as the Jewish widower Herr Schultz, presented another view of doomed romance and doomed humanity in a city symbolized by a night club and its sardonic Emcee (played by Joel Grey): "Come to the cabaret!" And audiences did -- for 1,165 performances.

During the course of the play Herr Schultz, the owner of a fruit shop, becomes engaged to Fraulein Schneider. His gifts are always fruit: Seville oranges in Act II, Scene 6, as the hero is packing to leave Berlin; a pineapple for Fraulein Schneider in Act I, Scene 7 ("If I could, I would fill your entire room with pineapples."). There is a sweet pathos in his efforts, which are eventually thwarted when Fraulein Schneider succumbs to Nazi warnings.

A GIFT OF FRUIT SALAD

For a party of 6.   Preparation time: about 15 minutes.

2 golden delicious apples, cored and cut into 3/4" chunks
2 ripe pears, cored and cut into 3/4" chunks

117

1 cup drained canned pineapple chunks
3/4 cup seedless grapes
1/4 cup drained, chopped maraschino cherries
1/4 cup shredded coconut
1/4 cup slivered almonds
2 bananas, cut into 1/2" slices
6 large leaves red or green leaf lettuce

Chill all the ingredients except the bananas and lettuce well in advance. In a large decorative bowl (we use a cut glass bowl), toss together all the ingredients except the lettuce. Arrange the lettuce on individual serving plates and top each with salad. Serve immediately with slices of raisin bread and a soft, spreadable cheese such as Gormandaise.

♫ YOU'RE A GOOD MAN, ♫ CHARLIE BROWN

Book, music and lyrics by Clark Gesner
Opened March 7, 1967, at Theatre 80 St. Marks

It is surprising that this musical ever got *into* a theatre, not to mention its run of 1,572 performances! According to Gesner, there was no script for the first rehearsal on February 2, 1967, -- only ten songs and a lot of people. On opening night there was still no script, but as Gesner explained, "nobody much cared." Described as "an average day in the life of Charlie Brown," the musical, obviously based on Charles Schultz's popular "Peanuts" comic strip, did not require much plot. Everyone knew the scenes and readily accepted the characters, as well as one popular song, "Happiness Is."

For "Peanuts" aficionados, there is only one appropriate food, and the musical mentions it quite early.

Charlie Brown (unwraps sandwich): Peanut butter. Some psychiatrists say that people who eat peanut butter sandwiches are lonely. I guess they're right. And if you're really lonely, the peanut butter sticks to the roof of your mouth.
Patty (to Linus): We had spaghetti at our house three times this week.

For a recipe for another long-running spaghetti, see page 50. Meanwhile, here is Charlie Brown's concoction.

CHARLIE BROWN'S LONELY PEANUT BUTTER SANDWICHES

Preparation time: about a minute per sandwich.

At least twice as many slices of inexpensive white bread as there are members in your party
A little margarine

119

A jar of smooth peanut butter
A jar of marshmallow fluff (<u>not</u> marshmallow creme!)

For the best peanut butter sandwich, you need to coat one slice of bread lightly with margarine before applying a whopping portion of peanut butter. On another piece of bread, spread an ample amount of marshmallow fluff. Then simply fit the two pieces together, and repeat the process with the other sandwiches. With a glass of milk, you have an unbeatable match -- if you are twelve or under (or maybe even, like us, a little over).

♫

More serious-minded cooks may enjoy Lucy's book report on *Peter Rabbit* and the following recipes for turnips and parsnips.

Peter Rabbit is this stupid book
About this stupid rabbit who steals
Vegetables from other people's gardens.
(Sings)
Lettuce and turnips and
Parsley and okra and cabbage
And string beans and parsnips,
Tomatoes, potatoes, asparagus,
Cauliflower, rhubarb and chives.

CREAMED TURNIPS

For a party of 6.   Preparation time: about 30 minutes.

6-8 medium turnips, peeled and cut into 1" cubes
2 tablespoons unsalted butter or margarine
1/2 cup half-and-half or milk
Salt and freshly ground black pepper, to taste
Sprigs of fresh parsley, for garnish

Bring enough water to cover the turnips to boil in a medium saucepan. Add the turnips and cook, uncovered, for 15-20 minutes, or until very tender. Drain the turnips, add the butter, half-and-half, salt and pepper and mash until smooth. Serve immediately, garnished with fresh parsley.

"FRENCH FRIED" PARSNIPS

For a party of 6. Preparation time: about 20 minutes.

8-10 young parsnips, peeled and cut into 1/2" strips
Extra virgin olive oil
Salt, to taste

Preheat the oven to 350°. Arrange the parsnips in a single layer on a well greased baking sheet. Drizzle with the oil. Bake for 15 minutes, or until golden. Sprinkle with salt and serve immediately. Even the peanuts in your family will like these parsnips!

For recipe for cabbage, see pages 168 and 174. For asparagus soup, see page 183.

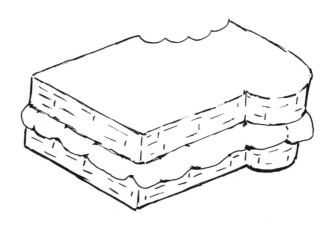

♫ HAIR ♫

Book and lyrics by Gerome Ragni and James Rado
Music by Galt MacDermot
Opened October 17, 1967, at the Anspacher Theatre

The production history of the epochal musical -- "The American Tribal Love-Rock Musical" -- is as exciting as its success. After a limited engagement of eight weeks at Joe Papp's New York Shakespeare Festival's Public Theatre, Papp moved the show, for another brief run, to Cheetah, a large Broadway discotheque. Then, revised by its authors and restaged by Tom O'Horgan, *Hair* opened at the Biltmore Theatre on April 29, 1968, and ran for 1,742 performances. Memorable for its rock score and sprinkling of nudity, the musical represented the rebellion of grown-up adolescents in a Marshall McLuhan world which has since become passé. As the archetypical musical of the Sixties, it became extremely popular, grossing $80 million and being performed in most countries of the world.

The freewheeling storyline of *Hair* includes comments on many interests of the Sixties: sex, drugs, money, religion and nudity. A recurring theme involves the character Claude, who does not want to be drafted. In Act II, he has made a decision: He will not go into the army tomorrow.

> Claude: Let's go to Mexico, George.
> Berger: I told you the <u>boogey man</u> would get you.
> Claude: I want to eat mushrooms and sleep in the sun.

CLAUDE'S MUSHROOMS

For a party of 6. Preparation time: about 20 minutes.

1 tablespoon unsalted butter or margarine
3 tablespoons extra virgin olive oil
1 teaspoon ground cumin
3 cups trimmed and sliced fresh mushrooms
Salt and freshly grated black pepper, to taste

In a large skillet over medium heat, melt the butter in the oil. Stir in the cumin. Add the mushrooms and sauté until the moisture has evaporated and the mushrooms are golden. Season with salt and pepper and serve immediately.

♫

Another constant character in *Hair* is Hud, "a colored spade." "If you ask him to dinner, feed him." (Act I.)

Hud: Watermelon
     Hominy Grits
     Alligator Ribs
     An' shortnin' Bread.

HUD'S HOMINY GRITS

For a party of 6. Preparation time: about 4 hours, plus soaking.

1 quart dried corn
2 tablespoons baking soda
1 teaspoon salt
Melted unsalted butter or margarine

Shell and wash the corn. In a stainless steel or enamel pan, cover the corn with 2 quarts of water. Add the baking soda, cover and let stand for 12 hours. Bring the corn to a boil in the soaking liquid. Reduce the heat to simmer and cook, uncovered, for about 3 hours, or until the hulls loosen, adding water if necessary. Drain the corn and plunge it into cold water. Rub the corn until the hulls are removed. Bring the corn to a boil in 2 quarts of cold water. Drain and rub again, place the corn in 2 quarts of cold water, add the salt and bring to a boil. Drain and serve immediately with the butter or margarine.

♫ ZORBÁ ♫

Book by Joseph Stein   Music by John Kander
Lyrics by Fred Ebb
Opened November 17, 1968, at the Imperial Theatre

To bring Nikos Kazantzakis' novel, *Zorbá the Greek*, to life on the stage, as well as capitalize on the popular 1965 movie starring Anthony Quinn, Harold Prince created a choral framework of musicians who act out and comment on the story of Zorbá, played by Herschel Bernardi. As one would expect from Kazantzakis, Zorbá's drama is one of somber substance rather than spectacle, and the struggle within Zorbá is that of intellect versus the human heart.

Zorbá is a thoughtful man, as he shows in Act II, Scene 5:

> The only real death is the death you die every day by not living. Oh, boss, what a strange machine man is, you fill him with bread, wine, fish, radishes, and out of him comes laughing, crying, loving . . . only if his soul is free."

Zorbá is also a man of flesh, of many appetites. He explains in Act I, Scene 2:

> I soar like a sea gull.
> I stamp like a bull.
> I comb out my whiskers so ladies can pull.
> I chew on the mutton
> Until my belly's full.

"Life is what you do while you're waiting to die," sings the leader of the chorus. Take advantage of it.

> Hungry for the pilaf
> In someone else's pot
> But that's the only choice you've got!

ZORBÁ'S SHISH KEBABS

For a party of 6.   Preparation time: about 45 minutes, plus chilling.

2 pounds lean lamb, cut into 1 1/2" cubes
1-2 cloves garlic, minced
1/2 cup extra virgin olive oil
Juice of 2 lemons
1 teaspoon salt
1/8 teaspoon freshly ground black pepper
2 teaspoons dried oregano
1 medium onion, sliced into rings
1 bay leaf
2 large green bell peppers, membranes and seeds removed,
    cut lengthwise into thirds
12 1 1/2" fresh mushroom caps (stems reserved for pilaf)
12 cherry tomatoes

Place the lamb in a shallow pan. In a small bowl, beat together the garlic, oil, lemon juice, salt, pepper and oregano. Pour the mixture over the meat. Add the onion and bay leaf, cover the pan and chill 3-4 hours.

Preheat the broiler or outdoor grill. Place the bell peppers in a pan of boiling water and blanch for 1 minute. Drain the peppers and cut each piece crosswise into thirds. On 6 skewers, alternate pieces of lamb, bell pepper, mushroom caps (lengthwise through stem ends) and tomatoes. Brush the kebabs with the marinade and broil or cook on the grill for 8-12 minutes, according to taste. Serve hot, with pilaf -- your very own! You do have a choice!

YOUR VERY OWN PILAF

For a party of 6.   Preparation time: about 1 hour.

1/3 cup plus 1 tablespoon unsalted butter or margarine
1/4 teaspoon dried rosemary

12 fresh mushroom stems
3 cups clear chicken stock
1/4 teaspoon dried sage
1/2 teaspoon salt
1 1/2 cups long grain rice, washed and drained

In a small saucepan, melt 1 tablespoon butter. Add the rosemary and mushroom stems and brown for about 4 minutes. In another pan, bring the stock to a boil and add the sage and salt. In a large saucepan, melt the remaining butter. Add the rice and cook over medium heat for 5-6 minutes, or until the butter is absorbed. Add the stock, a bit at a time, stirring constantly. Cover and simmer for 15 minutes. Add the rosemary, butter and mushroom stems. Reduce heat to low and cook, stirring constantly, for about 4 minutes. Remove from the heat, cover and let stand for about 25 minutes before serving.

Other recipes for lamb (pretend it's mutton!) appear on pages 174 and 185.

♫ **PROMISES, PROMISES** ♫

Book by Neil Simon   Music by Burt Bacharach
Lyrics by Hal David
Opened December 1, 1968, at the Shubert Theatre

Jerry Orbach played Chuck Baxter, the affable and somewhat spineless, yet ambitious, young man whose popularity with his bosses is directly proportionate to his generosity in making his nearby apartment available for their extramarital daylight dalliances. Mainly, however, Chuck gets only promises . . . promises. A complication arises when Fran, played by Jill O'Hara, reacts badly to her role in the game the bosses play and is romantically rescued by Chuck. From the Bacharach and David score, Fran's wistful "What Do You Get When You Fall in Love?" is a real show-stopper. Based on Billy Wilder and I. A. L. Diamond's screenplay, *The Apartment*, the musical ran for 1,281 performances.

Because Chuck has restricted use of his apartment and Fran becomes a hostess in the Executive Dining Room, there is a considerable amount of dining out in the show. In Act I, Scene 6, Fran complains that one of the bosses, Mr. Sheldrake, who once showed an interest in her, has "gone from 'I love you, Fran,' to 'How are the scallops today?'" in two short months.

SCALLOPS TODAY

For a party of 6.   Preparation time: about 1 hour.

2 1/2 cups fresh bay scallops
2 tablespoons unsalted butter or margarine
1/4 cup diced onion
1/4 cup diced green bell pepper
1/4 cup flour

1-2 teaspoons dry mustard
Freshly grated black pepper, to taste
2 cups milk
1 1/2 cups grated cheddar cheese
6 ounces condensed tomato soup
1/2 cup chopped stuffed olives
1 cup fine bread crumbs

Preheat the oven to 350°. In a saucepan, cover the scallops with cold water and bring to a boil over high heat. Reduce the heat to simmer and cook 5 minutes. Drain and set aside. Melt the butter in a large skillet. Add the onion and bell pepper and sauté until the onion is translucent. Stir in the flour, mustard and black pepper. Add the milk a bit at a time and stir constantly until the mixture thickens. Stir in the cheese, soup, olives and scallops. Place the mixture in a baking dish that has been sprayed with non-stick spray. Sprinkle the bread crumbs evenly over the mixture. Bake for about 25 minutes. Serve immediately.

♬

In the next scene, Chuck enters the Dining Room and sees Fran, who has rejected his invitation to go to a ball game because she was with Sheldrake (who had set up the situation himself by giving Chuck tickets to the game). In an awkward attempt to make conversation, Chuck asks: "How's the Chicken Pot Pie?"

EXECUTIVE STYLE CHICKEN POT PIE

For a party of 6-8. Preparation time: about 1 hour.

For the crust:
3/4 cup milk
1 tablespoon white wine vinegar
2 cups unbleached flour, plus extra flour for dusting

2 teaspoons baking powder
1 teaspoon baking soda
1/2 teaspoon (or less) salt
5 tablespoons unsalted butter or margarine

For the filling:
1 1/2 cups chicken stock
12 small onions
4 tablespoons unsalted butter or margarine
3 tablespoons unbleached flour
2 cups milk
1 tablespoon chopped fresh parsley
4 cups cubed cooked chicken

Make the crust: Preheat the oven to 450°. In a small bowl, combine the milk and vinegar and let stand. Into a large bowl, sift together the flour, baking powder, baking soda and salt. Cut in the butter, using a pastry cutter or two knives. Pour in the milk and stir quickly. The dough will form a sticky mass. Working quickly, turn out the dough onto a well-floured surface and pat into a 3/4" thickness. With a bisquit or cookie cutter, cut the dough into circles or other shapes.

In a saucepan, bring the stock to a gentle boil. Add the onions, reduce the heat to simmer, cover and cook for about 10 minutes.   Drain and set aside the onions, reserving the stock.

Heat the butter in a large skillet over medium heat. Add the flour and stir to blend thoroughly. Add the milk a bit at a time, stirring constantly until the mixture thickens. Stir in the parsley, chicken and onions. Pour the mixture into a baking dish that has been sprayed with non-stick spray. Arrange the crust cut-outs evenly on top of the filling and bake 15-20 minutes.   Allow the pie to cool for about 5 minutes before serving.

♫

The plot has progressed considerably by Act II, Scene 2, when Chuck, having rescued Fran from attempted suicide in his apartment, is confronted by her brother with questions concerning the presence of the doctor from next door. "Fruit cake," Chuck explains, "Too much fruitcake." Be moderate -- it could happen.

SUICIDE FRUITCAKE

For a party of 20-25. Preparation time: about 1 hour and 30 minutes.

1 cup dates
2 cups shelled pecans
1 cup unsalted butter or margarine
3/4 cup light brown sugar
5 eggs or 10 ounces egg substitute
2 cups unbleached flour
1/2 tablespoon salt
1 1/2 teaspoons baking powder
1/4 cup unsweetened pineapple juice
8 ounces candied red cherries
8 ounces candied green cherries
8 ounces candied pineapple
1 1/2 cups golden raisins
1 cup grated coconut

Preheat the oven to 275°. Chop the dates and pecans into large pieces and set aside. In a large bowl, cream the butter and sugar. Blend in the eggs. Add the flour, salt, baking powder and pineapple juice and blend thoroughly. Stir in the candied fruit, raisins and coconut. Place the batter in a greased 10" tube pan and bake for about 1 hour. Allow to cool before slicing.

♫ DAMES AT SEA ♫

Book by George Haimsohn and Robin Miller
Music by Jim Wise
Opened December 20, 1968, at the Bouwerie Lane Theatre

First performed at the Caffe Cino in the Village, *Dames at Sea* poked good-natured fun at the old Dick Powell-Ruby Keeler movies. Bernadette Peters first attracted critical attention as Ruby, a dancer who, just off the bus from Utah, wants to be in a Broadway show. After 575 performances, *Dames at Sea* also had a good run at the Plaza Music Hall and opened in London on August 27, 1969, for 117 performances.

As you might expect, Ruby has both friends and foes in her climb to stardom. Mona Kent (born Grace Topolovsky), the reigning star, does not look favorably upon the ambitious Ruby; Joan and Jacky, however, wear white hats.

> Joan: Psst, Jacky, I want you to help me try out a recipe for cooking a goose.
> Jacky: Whose?
> Joan: Grace Topolovsky's, that's whose. It's time that peacock laid an egg.

Our recipe may not be exactly like the one Joan and Jackie try out, but it's better for the digestion.

A RECIPE FOR COOKING A GOOSE

For a party of 6-8.   Preparation time: about 5 hours.

For the stuffing:
1 loaf white or whole grain bread, torn into 1" pieces
1 pan cornbread, crumbled
1 large onion, chopped
1 stalk celery, chopped
2 eggs or 4 ounces egg substitute

1 teaspoon dried rosemary
1/4 teaspoon salt
1/2 teaspoon freshly ground black pepper

1 10-12 pound goose, washed and patted dry
2 tablespoons unsalted butter or margarine, melted
1 can cream of mushroom soup, undiluted

For the gravy:
2 cups clear chicken stock
1 tablespoon butter or margarine, melted
1 tablespoon flour
Salt and freshly ground black pepper, to taste

In a large bowl, combine the bread, cornbread, onion, celery, eggs, rosemary, salt and pepper. Loosely stuff the goose's cavity. (Any extra stuffing may be baked separately during the final 30 minutes before serving.) Lace the openings with string and tie the legs and wings close to the body. Insert a meat thermometer into the thick part of the breast, avoiding the bone. Do not stuff the goose more than a few minutes before roasting!

Preheat the oven to 300°. Brush the goose with the melted butter and place, breast side up, on a rack in a roasting pan. Pour 3 cups of hot water into the pan, cover and bake for 2 hours, adding more water if necessary. Remove the goose from the oven and trim off as much fat as possible. Pour the soup over the goose. Bake for 2 hours, basting every 15 minutes. Remove the goose from the pan and allow to stand for 15 minutes before carving.

Make the gravy: Discard the excess fat from the pan. Pour the stock into the pan, scraping to loosen any clinging bits. In a skillet, combine the butter and flour to make a paste. Gradually add the stock, stirring constantly. When the gravy thickens, season with salt and pepper.

♫ 1776 ♫

Book by Peter Stone
Music and lyrics by Sherman Edwards
Opened March 16, 1969, at the Forty-Sixth Street Theatre

Personal feuding and regional animosities among the delegates provide the human drama in this musical about the signing of the Declaration of Independence. Although no memorable songs linger, 1776 won the Drama Critics' Circle Award for Best Musical and ran for 1,217 performances.

Should they write a declaration? That question bothers the delegates who sit around Thomas Jefferson's room as he attempts to write. Finally, Ben Franklin speaks:

> Franklin: Well -- good night, John.
> Adams: Have y' eaten, Franklin?
> Franklin: Not yet, but --
> Adams: I hear the turkey's fresh at the Bunch o' Grapes.
> Franklin: I have a rendezvous, John.

History tells us that Ben Franklin enjoyed many rendezvous and that he was more recognized in the back streets of Paris than on the major thoroughfares. It also reminds us that he favored the turkey over the bald eagle as the symbol of America, finding the turkey native to the country and with a "much more respectable character."

BUNCH O' GRAPES TURKEY

For a party of 8-10. Preparation time: about 4 hours and 45 minutes.

1 10-pound turkey, giblets reserved, washed and patted dry
1 clove garlic, cut into thin slivers
1-2 tablespoons unsalted butter or margarine

For the stuffing:
1 loaf white bread, torn into 1" pieces
1 pan cornbread, crumbled
1 large onion, chopped
2 eggs or 4 ounces egg substitute
1 teaspoon dried sage
1/2 teaspoon salt
1/2 teaspoon freshly ground black pepper
2 cups sliced fresh mushrooms

For basting:
1/2 cup clear chicken stock

For the gravy:
2 cups clear chicken stock
Giblets from the turkey
1 tablespoon butter or margarine
1 large onion, finely chopped
1 tablespoon flour
2 hard boiled eggs, coarsely chopped
Salt and freshly ground black pepper, to taste

Preheat the oven to 450°. Cut several 1" slits in the skin of the turkey's breast, thighs and drumsticks and insert the garlic slivers, working well under the skin. Rub the turkey thoroughly with the butter.

In a large bowl, combine the bread, cornbread, onion, eggs, sage, salt, pepper and mushrooms. Stuff the turkey's cavity loosely with stuffing. (Extra stuffing may be baked separately during the final 30 minutes before serving.) Lace the openings with string and tie the legs and wings close to the body. Insert a meat thermometer into the thick part of the breast, avoiding the bone. Do not stuff the turkey more than a few minutes before of roasting!

Place the turkey, breast side up, on a rack in a roasting pan and roast, uncovered, for about 20 minutes, or until the skin is golden brown. Cover the turkey loosely with a foil tent, reduce the heat to 325° and roast for 20-25 minutes per pound, basting every 15 minutes, first with the 1/2 cup chicken stock, then with drippings from the pan.

About 1 hour before serving, begin the gravy: Place the 2 cups of stock in a saucepan and bring to a simmer. Add the giblets and cook, stirring occasionally. In a skillet over medium-low heat, melt the butter. Add the onion and sauté until translucent, about 10-15 minutes. Stir in the flour and cook until golden.

When your meat thermometer reaches 185° and the juices run clear when the thigh is pierced, the turkey is done. (The stuffing in the cavity should reach at least 165°.) Remove the turkey from the pan and allow to stand about 15 minutes before carving.

While the turkey stands, finish the gravy: Discard the excess fat from the roasting pan. Add about 1/2 cup of water to the pan, stirring and scraping to loosen all clinging bits from the sides of the pan. Pour the water, a bit at a time, into the skillet, stirring constantly. Stir in the giblets and their cooking liquid, the hard boiled eggs, salt and pepper. Stir constantly until the gravy thickens. Spoon liberally over the sliced turkey and stuffing.

♫

In Act I, Scene 5, as Congress is in session, Samuel Chase, the delegate from Maryland, is absorbed in his meal of kidneys, while others try to persuade him to vote "yea" for independence. Obviously, first things first with Mr. Chase.

SAMUEL CHASE'S STEAK AND KIDNEY PIE

For a party of 6. Preparation time: about 2 hours and 15 minutes

For the filling:
1/4 cup flour
1/2 teaspoon salt

1/4 teaspoon freshly ground black pepper
1 pound beef round steak, cut into 3/4" - 1" cubes
1 beef kidney, washed, tubes and fat removed, cubed (3/4")
3 tablespoons canola or safflower oil
1 medium onion, chopped
1/4 cup chopped pimiento
2 tablespoons Worcestershire sauce
1/2 teaspoon dried thyme

For the crust:
1 cup unbleached flour
1 teaspoon vegetable shortening
1/4 teaspoon salt

Place the flour, salt and pepper in a bag, add the steak and kidney and shake the bag to coat evenly. Reserve the extra flour. Heat the oil in a skillet over medium-high heat. Add the steak and kidney and brown evenly on all sides. Remove the steak and kidney, add the onion to the skillet and sauté until golden. Pour off the drippings and add the pimiento, Worcestershire sauce, thyme and 1 1/2 cups of water. Bring to a boil. Return the steak and kidney to the skillet and stir in the reserved flour. Reduce the heat to simmer and cook while you make the crust.

In a large bowl, combine the flour, shortening, salt and enough water to make a manageable dough. On a well floured surface, roll out the dough into a circle about 1/8" thick. Invert a 9" pie pan over the dough and cut a circle about 1" larger than the rim of the pan. Cut a second circle inside the first, about 1" from the edge. Moisten the edge of the pan with a bit of water and line the edge with the outer ring of dough. Place the steak and kidney filling in the pie pan. Top the pie with the remaining dough. Seal the edges of the crust with your fingers or a fork. Pierce the top crust several times with the fork. Bake for about 1 hour and 30 minutes. Serve immediately.

♫ PURLIE ♫

Book by Ossie Davis   Music by Gary Geld
Lyrics by Peter Udell
Opened March 15, 1970, at the Broadway Theatre

As the musical version of Ossie Davis' *Purlie Victorious*, 1961, this outrageously satirical perception of race relations in an unreconstructed South was much more successful than the play or the movie adaptation, *Gone Are the Days* (1963). All characters, black and white, are presented with humor, as they live their lives in the county of Big Bethel, somewhere in South Georgia. In the premiere production, Clevon Little played Purlie and Melba Moore played Lutiebelle.

The tone of the musical is set in Act I, Scene 1, as Lutiebelle reminisces:

> Oh, Aunt Missy, this puts me in mind of all the good things I ever had in my life. Picnics, fish-fries, corn-shuckings, and love-feasts, and gospel-singing; picking huckleberries, roasting groundpeas, quilting-bee parties and barbeques; that kind of . . . Welcome! you can't get nowhere else in all this world.

To celebrate some of life's good things, we offer a recipe for barbeque:

BARBEQUED BEEF

For a party of 8. Preparation time: about 20 minutes, plus marinating.

Juice of 1-2 lemons
3/4 cup light soy sauce
1/2 cup dry red wine

4 tablespoons canola or safflower oil
4 tablespoons Worcestershire sauce
2 large cloves garlic, thinly sliced
Freshly ground black pepper, to taste
1/2 cup chopped scallions
2 tablespoons chopped fresh dill weed
2 1 1/2-pound flank steaks, excess fat removed

In a large flat bowl or pan, mix the lemon juice, soy sauce, wine, oil, Worcestershire sauce, garlic, pepper, scallions and dill weed. Marinate the steaks in the mixture, turning occasionally, for 3-12 hours -- in the refrigerator.

Heat an outdoor grill. For rare meat, cook for 5 minutes on each side. Slice the meat diagonally across the grain and serve immediately.

For a recipe for fried fish, see page 25.

♬

In Act II, Scene 1, Purlie uses food to make comparisons:

> [The white man] could wax hisself fat on the fat of the land: steaks, rice, chicken, roastineers, sweet potato pies, hot buttered bisquits and corn syrup anytime he felt like and never hit a lick at a snake! And us got to every day get-up-and-git-with-it, sunup-to-sundown, on fatback and cornmeal hoecakes . . . and don't wind up owning enough ground to get buried standing up in!

For steaks, see page 53; for rice, 98 and 125; for chicken, 6, 37, 105, 154 and 158; for "roastineers," 11; and for sweet potato pie, 21.

♫ APPLAUSE ♫

Book by Betty Comden and Adolf Greene
Music by Charles Strouse   Lyrics by Lee Adams
Opened March 30, 1970, at the Palace Theatre

Backstage backstabbing is the order of the day in this adaptation of the film *All About Eve.* As Margo Channing, the ex-glamour queen caught in conflict with her unscrupulously ambitious protegée, Eve Harrington, Lauren Bacall was described as a "sensation." Penny Fuller played Eve in a cast that included Len Cariou and Alan King. In the end their efforts won five Tony Awards and a run of 896 performances before Lauren Bacall repeated her role at Her Majesty's Theatre in London.

In Act II, Scene 4, Bill (Len Cariou) thinks of Margo as "One of a Kind."

> Bill: And you're the kind of woman for me!
>   Who else would take a swim completely dressed
>   In Central Park at three A. M.
>   The night she won the Tony?   ·
> Margo: Who grabbed a flaming cherries jubilee
>   And burned a movie script at Chasen's
>   Yelling it was phony!

FLAMING CHERRIES JUBILEE

For a party of 4.   Preparation time: about 15 minutes.

1 16-ounce can pitted tart bing cherries
Zest of 1 lemon, grated
1/4 cup plus 3 tablespoons sugar
1/4 teaspoon ground cinnamon
3-4 tablespoons plus 1/2 cup cognac
1 tablespoon cornstarch

Drain the cherries and reserve the liquid. In a medium bowl gently toss the cherries, lemon zest, 1/4 cup sugar, the cinnamon and 3-4 tablespoons cognac. Let stand for a few minutes.

Remove the cherries from the bowl and set aside. Add the cornstarch to the remaining contents of the bowl and blend thoroughly. Stir in 3-4 tablespoons of the reserved liquid from the can. Pour the mixture into a chafing dish pan and stir over medium heat until thickened, about 5-6 minutes. Stir in the cherries and heat thoroughly, adding more reserved liquid as needed.

In a small saucepan, warm the remaining 1/2 cup cognac.

To serve, place the chafing dish pan over a flame, sprinkle the cherries with the remaining sugar and add the warm cognac. Heat and, touching carefully with a lighted match, set aflame. When the flame dies down, spoon the cherries over bowls of vanilla ice cream.

♫

Two scenes later, Eve's treachery -- passing out "favors" to the right people to steal a role from Margo -- has come to light, and a new dawn breaks for Margo. She turns to a friend -- "Karen, got a good recipe for lasagne?" -- and then sings "Something Greater." The ego war is over; Margo has Bill back. "Eve," she says, "you four-star bitch! Thank you!" Something greater; "That's for me!" And for us, too!

A GREATER LASAGNE

For a party of 6-8. Preparation time: about 2 hours.

1 pound extra lean ground beef
1 large onion, peeled and finely chopped

2-3 cloves garlic, peeled and minced
1/2 cup sliced fresh mushrooms
1 green bell pepper, membranes and seeds removed,
    chopped
1 tablespoon tomato paste
1 28-ounce can crushed or ground tomatoes in their liquid
1 bay leaf
1 teaspoon dried oregano
1 teaspoon dried basil
1 teaspoon dried Italian parsley
1 teaspoon chili powder
1/2 cup red wine
1 box lasagne noodles
1/2 cup chopped pitted ripe olives
1 cup ricotta cheese
1 cup shredded mozzarella cheese

In a very large skillet, brown the ground beef over
medium heat. Add the onion, garlic, mushrooms and
bell pepper and cook for about 10 minutes. Add the
tomato paste, tomatoes in their liquid, bay leaf, oregano,
basil, Italian parsley and chili powder. Raise the heat to
bring to a boil. Immediately reduce the heat to simmer,
cover and cook for at least 1 hour. Stir in the wine and
cook, uncovered, for 5-10 minutes.

While the sauce simmers, cook the lasagne according to
package directions and preheat the oven to 350°. When
the sauce is done, remove the bay leaf from the sauce and
spread a light layer of sauce in the bottom of a large
rectangular baking dish. Arrange the ingredients in the
baking dish in several layers, in the following order:
noodles, sauce, a sprinkling of olives, several dollops of
ricotta, a sprinkling of mozzarella (being sure to reserve
enough mozzarella to give the top layer a generous
amount). Bake for 25-30 minutes. Serve immediately.

♫ COMPANY ♫

Book by George Furth
Music and lyrics by Stephen Sondheim
Opened April 26, 1970, at the Alvin Theatre

First conceived as a series of one-act plays on the subject of marriage, *Company* became vignettes emphasizing, according to Sondheim, "the total possibility and impossibility" of relationships on the island of Manhattan. Neither Sondheim nor Harold Prince, the producer, however, ever satisfactorily answered the question: "Is *Company* for or against marriage?" John Lahr called *Company* "an urban ghost dance." Others have compared George Furth's Manhattan to Woody Allen's but noted Furth's lack of compassion for his bewildered characters. Prince is credited with relieving some of the story's black humor, and Elaine Stritch was a hit as Joanne in the New York production and in London.

People do eat in Manhattan. In the opening number, Robert, played by Dean Jones, is invited for dinner, "Eight O'clock on Monday." "Bobby, come on over for dinner! We'll be so glad to see you!" Unfortunately, we never discover what they eat -- the emphasis is always on "Company! Lots of company! Life is company! Love is company!"

In the song entitled "Side by Side by Side," Robert becomes the center of attention, and we find the only reference to a specific dish:

> What would we do without you?
> How would we ever get through?
> Who would I complain to for hours?
> Who'd bring all the flowers, When I have the flu?
> Who'd finish yesterday's stew?
> Who'd take the kids to the zoo?

Robert, it seems, does many things for these good and crazy people -- his married friends -- and, in return, he gets . . .

YESTERDAY'S STEW

For a party of 6. Preparation time: about 2 hours, including simmering.

3 tablespoons flour
1 teaspoon ground cumin
1 pound lean stew beef, cut into 1" chunks
2 tablespoons canola, safflower or corn oil
Salt and freshly ground black pepper, to taste
1 clove garlic, minced
10-12 new potatoes in their jackets, cut into 3/4" - 1"
    chunks
8-10 carrots, scraped and cut into 3/4" chunks
6-8 small onions, halved or quartered

Place the flour and cumin in a bag, add the beef and shake the bag until the beef is evenly coated. Heat the oil in a large skillet over medium heat, add the meat and cook, turning frequently, until brown on all sides. Add the salt, pepper and garlic and cook for about 3 minutes more.

Meanwhile, bring 6 cups of cold water to a boil in a large pot. Add the beef, reduce the heat to simmer, cover and cook for 1 hour and 15 minutes, or until the meat is very tender. Add the potatoes, carrots and onions and cook, uncovered, for 20-25 minutes, or until the potatoes are tender but not mushy. Serve immediately or refrigerate overnight and reheat -- for "company."

♫ GREASE ♫

Book, music and lyrics by Jim Jacobs and Warren Casey
Opened February 14, 1972, at the Eden Theatre
Transferred June 71, 1972, to the Broadhurst Theatre

A nostalgic view of the "greaser" young people of the 1950's, who made a cult of leather jackets and bouffant hairstyles, this "rock n' roll" musical has become a popular-culture landmark and has been compared to the film *American Graffiti*. Originally written for a community theatre in Chicago, *Grease* found an appreciative audience in New York, where it stayed for 3,388 performances, featuring Carole Demas and Barry Bostwick. Perhaps indicative of its completely American character, it lasted for only 258 performances in London.

Act I, Scene 2, takes place on the first day of school at Rydell High. As the Pink Ladies assemble for lunch in the cafeteria, Jan adds a plate of coleslaw to her already overloaded tray. The meal, predictably, does not go smoothly. Overly conscious of her new glasses, Marty asks if they make her look smarter.

> Rizzo: Nah, we can still see your face.
> Marty: How'dja like rice pudding down your bra?

Sandy, the newcomer, thinks the coleslaw "smells kinda funny," and the comment describing the chipped beef has no place in a cookbook. Nor does Marty's language when she realizes that "one of her diamonds fell in the macaroni." The food, however, is worthy of attention.

RYDELL RICE PUDDING

For a party of 6. Preparation time: about 1 hour.

1 cup white rice
4 eggs or 8 ounces egg substitute
2 tablespoons flour

1 cup sugar
1 1/2 cups milk
1 teaspoon pure vanilla extract

In a large pan, bring the rice and 2 cups of cold water to a boil, uncovered, over high heat. Immediately reduce the heat to simmer, cover and cook for 15 minutes. Remove from the heat and allow to stand, covered, for 5 minutes.

While the rice cooks, preheat the oven to 350°. Place the eggs in the top of a double boiler. Mix the flour into the sugar and stir, a bit at a time, into the eggs. Add 1/2 cup of milk and stir to blend thoroughly. Blend in the remaining milk. Cook, stirring constantly, over boiling water until the mixture thickens. Remove from the heat and let stand for about 5 minutes. Stir in the vanilla extract. Add the rice and mix well. Place the rice mixture in a buttered baking dish and bake, uncovered, for 30 minutes. Serve with the following sauce.

1/2 cup unsalted butter or margarine
1 cup sugar
2 eggs or 4 ounces egg substitute
3/4 cup dry sherry
Zest of 1 lemon, grated
Grating fresh nutmeg, to taste

Cream the butter and sugar. Beat the eggs and stir into the butter mixture. Add the sherry, lemon zest and nutmeg. Pour the sauce into the top of a double boiler and beat over boiling water until heated through. Serve hot.

PINK LADY COLESLAW

For a party of 6. Preparation time: about 20 minutes, plus chilling.

2 tablespoons sugar
1/4 teaspoon (or less) salt
2 teaspoons celery seeds
2 tablespoons vinegar

2 teaspoons Dijon mustard
1/4 cup mayonnaise
1 head cabbage, shredded or chopped
1/2 cup green bell pepper, julienne cut
1 small red onion, halved and cut into very thin slices
Freshly ground black pepper, to taste

In a large bowl, mix together the sugar, salt, celery seeds, vinegar, mustard and mayonnaise. Add, a bit at a time, the cabbage, bell pepper and onion, tossing to mix thoroughly after each addition. Mix in fresh black pepper to taste. Chill thoroughly before serving.

MACARONI AND CHEESE

For a party of 6.   Preparation time: about 1 hour.

1 tablespoon extra virgin olive oil
1 pound penne or ziti
1 clove garlic, peeled and split lengthwise
Unsalted butter or margarine, for the baking dish
5 cups milk
1/4 teaspoon salt
Freshly ground black pepper, to taste
Grating of fresh nutmeg
1 cup half-and-half
2 cups grated Swiss cheese
3 tablespoons unsalted butter, broken into small pieces

To a large pot of rapidly boiling water, add the olive oil and pasta. Cook for 6-7 minutes. Drain but do not rinse.

Preheat the oven to 350°.   Rub a large baking dish with the garlic, then generously spread with the butter. In a large pan, heat the milk and stir in the salt, pepper and nutmeg. Mix together the half-and-half and pasta and pour into the baking dish. Top with the cheese and dot with the butter. Bake for 45 minutes. Serve immediately.

♫ THE CONTRAST ♫

Book by Anthony Stimac   Music by Don Pippin
Lyrics by Steve Brown
Opened November 27, 1972, at the East Side Playhouse

The Contrast, the original play from which this musical was adapted, is generally recognized as the first professionally staged comedy written by an American -- Royall Tyler. It opened on April 16, 1787, at the John Street Theatre in New York. As a play and as a musical comedy, *The Contrast* owes much to Richard Brinsley Sheridan's *The School for Scandal* and to the creation of a country bumpkin, Jonathan, whose career on the stage is still promoted by American playwrights.

The music is lively, even in the eighteenth century play, while superimposed over everything is contrast -- contrast between England and America, between city and country, between hypocrisy and sincerity, between foreign fraud and native worth. A true-blue American, Jonathan sings a familiar ditty in the third act.

> Father and I went up to camp,
> Along with Captain Goodwin;
> And there we saw the men and boys
> As thick as hasty pudding.
> Yankee Doodle keep it up . . .

And in case you've always wondered just how thick hasty pudding really is . . .

HASTY PUDDING

For a party of 6.   Preparation time: about 30 minutes.

8 slices white bread
4 eggs or 8 ounces egg substitute
1 cup sugar
4 cups milk

1 teaspoon pure vanilla extract
2 tablespoons cinnamon-sugar mixture, for topping

Preheat the oven to 350°.   Tear the bread into 1" pieces and place in a well greased baking dish. In a separate bowl, beat together the eggs, sugar and milk. Stir in the vanilla extract.   Pour the egg mixture evenly over the bread. Sprinkle with the cinnamon-sugar mixture. Bake for 20 minutes, or until golden brown.

♫ A LITTLE NIGHT MUSIC ♫

Book by Hugh Wheeler
Music and lyrics by Stephen Sondheim
Opened February 25, 1973, at the Shubert Theatre

Director and producer Harold Prince is usually given credit for the success of *A Little Night Music*, but a cast including Glynis Johns, Len Cariou and Hermione Gingold helped it achieve a Tony for Best Musical and the Drama Critics' Circle Award. Set in turn-of-the-century Sweden, this adaptation of Ingmar Bergman's film, *Smiles of a Summer Night*, measured the sophisticated game-playing of interchanging romantic partners in variations of three-quarter waltz time music. In his movie version, Prince cast Elizabeth Taylor as Desirée but lost the artistry of the Broadway musical, according to Hermione Gingold, who didn't understand why the film was shot in Vienna when the scene was "Denmark, or one of those cold places."

On the stage in Act I, Scene 6, lemonade and cookies, properly presented by a servant named Petra, suggest an affected aloofness that can be quite theatrical.

> Anne: Lemonade, Charlotte?
> Charlotte: Lemonade! It would choke me! (sings)
> Every day a little death/ . . . I think love's a dirty business.

Still, on your own porch, a glass of lemonade reinforced with some cookies can be both comforting and refreshing.

LEMONADE

For a large party. Preparation time: about 1 hour.

2 cups sugar
Zest of 2 lemons, grated
1/8 teaspoon (or less) salt
Juice of 6 lemons

In a saucepan, combine the sugar, zest and salt. Stir in 1 cup of boiling water. Allow the mixture to cool and add the lemon juice. Strain the mixture through a sieve. Add 2 tablespoons of the lemonade mixture to each glass of ice water, seltzer or club soda. (For smaller parties, leftover mixture may be stored in a covered glass container.)

SWEDISH CREAM-FILLED COOKIES

Makes about 1 dozen cookies. Preparation time: about 30 minutes, plus chilling and cooling.

For the cookies:
1 cup unsalted butter, softened
1/3 cup heavy cream or whipping cream
2 cups unbleached flour
Sugar

For the filling:
1/4 cup unsalted butter, softened
3/4 cup sifted confectioners sugar
1 ounce egg substitute
1 teaspoon pure vanilla extract

In a medium bowl, mix together the butter and cream. Stir in the flour. Chill the mixture for about 1 hour.

Preheat the oven to 375°. Roll out the chilled dough to a thickness of about 1/2". Cut rounds with a 1 1/2" cookie cutter. Sprinkle a sheet of waxed paper liberally with sugar and place the cookies on the paper to coat with sugar. Turn with a spatula, making sure both sides are coated. Arrange the cookies on an ungreased cookie sheet and bake for 7-9 minutes. Cool on racks.

While the cookies cool, make the filling: Blend the butter, confectioners sugar, egg substitute and vanilla extract until smooth and creamy. Spread the filling evenly on half of the cookies and top with the other half.

♫ THE WIZ ♫

Book by William F. Brown
Music and lyrics by Charlie Smalls
Opened January 5, 1975, at the Majestic Theatre

Featuring an all-black cast (headed by Stephanie Mills as Dorothy), *The Wiz* retells L. Frank Baum's story of Oz in jive talk interlaced with rock, gospel and soul music. Marvelously energetic and spectacularly colorful, it was described by critics as picturesque, vivid, exotic and charming. Not surprisingly, it ran for 1,672 performances and received seven Tony Awards, including one for Best Musical.

Having followed the Yellow Brick Road out of the Land of the Munchkins, Dorothy finds herself in a cornfield, frightened by crows. It is Act I, Scene 2, and while the crows feast on the ears of corn, the Scarecrow appears. We suggest that you play the role of the Scarecrow and rescue the crop . . . for chowder!

CORNFIELD CHOWDER

For a party of 6.   Preparation time: about 45 minutes.

2 thin slices salt pork
2 tablespoons corn oil
1 large onion, thinly sliced
1/2 cup red or green bell pepper, thinly sliced
2 tablespoons flour
2 cups finely diced new potatoes, skins on
1/4 teaspoon salt
2 cups cooked corn
2 1/2 cups milk
Freshly ground black pepper, to taste

In a very large skillet or pot, cook the salt pork over medium-high heat to remove the excess fat. Discard the excess fat and drain the pork on paper towels. Add the corn oil to the skillet and heat. Add the onion and bell pepper and sauté until the onion is translucent. Add the flour and stir until golden. While the flour browns, bring 1 1/2 cups of water to a boil. Add the water, potatoes and salt to the skillet and cook, uncovered, for 10-12 minutes. Add the corn and milk and bring just to the scalding point (do not boil!) Season to taste with freshly ground pepper and serve immediately with oyster crackers.

If you prefer corn-on-the-cob, a recipe appears on page 11.

In Act I, Scene 5, the Wiz produces a large box marked "All Bran." "All Brain," he explains to the Scarecrow:

> . . . through the miracle of modern science, they have dehydrated, pre-frozen, and packaged a distillation of some of the best brains in the world. We're going to restuff your head with this!

And so he does, making the Scarecrow "suave, sophisticated, and self-assured." We make no such claims for our muffins, although we may assume.

THE WIZ'S ALL-BRAIN MUFFINS

Makes 10-18 muffins, depending upon the size of the tin. Preparation time: about 35 minutes.

1 egg
2 tablespoons unsalted butter or margarine, melted
1/2 cup molasses or maple syrup
3/4 cup milk
1 cup unbleached flour

1 teaspoon baking powder
1/2 teaspoon baking soda
1/4 teaspoon (or less) salt
1/2 cup golden raisins
1 cup bran flakes

Preheat the oven to 350°. In a large bowl, beat the egg. Add the butter and molasses and mix well. Add the milk. Sift together the flour, baking powder, baking soda and salt and stir into the egg mixture. Stir in the raisins and bran flakes. Place the mixture in well-greased tins and bake for about 20 minutes. Serve warm.

♬ SHENANDOAH ♬

Book by James Lee Barrett   Music by Gary Geld
Lyrics by Peter Udell
Opened January 7, 1975, at the Alvin Theatre

Originally staged at the Goodspeed Opera House in East Haddam, Connecticut, this period piece about a peaceful Virginia farmer who is drawn into the chaos of the Civil War presented a sharp contrast to many of the musicals of the Seventies. Forthright and guileless, *Shenandoah* emphasized the values of self-reliance, patriotism, a united family of mankind and wholesome living. As stated in Act II, Scene 5, "North or South, they're all our children." Audiences evidently appreciated the spirit of the musical and kept it on Broadway for more than two years.

Like all generations, the farmer's sons have their dreams. James and his wife, Anne, sing of the home they want in "Violets and Silverbells" (Act II, Scene 1):

    Anne: With our own parlor.
    James: And our own porch with a breeze from the
       mountains.
    Anne: And pots and pans and chicken on Sunday.
    James: And a bed with two left sides.

The bed may present a problem, but the chicken is easily managed.

SOUTHERN SUNDAY CHICKEN

For a party of 4-6.   Preparation time: about 1 hour.

1/2 cup flour
1/4 teaspoon freshly ground black pepper
A pinch of cayenne pepper

1 fryer, cut into serving pieces (skin may be removed to
    reduce fat)
2 slices thick cut bacon, cut into 1/2" squares
1/4 cup (or more) safflower, canola or corn oil
1 medium onion, coarsely chopped
1 1/2 cups sliced fresh mushrooms
1 cup milk
Salt and freshly ground black pepper, to taste
Paprika

Mix together the flour, 1/4 teaspoon black pepper and the
cayenne pepper. Dredge the chicken lightly in the flour
mixture, coating evenly on all sides. Set the chicken aside
and reserve the excess flour.

In a large skillet over medium heat, cook the bacon until
almost crisp. Remove the bacon from the skillet and blot
on paper towels to remove excess fat. Discard any fat
remaining in the skillet. Add the oil to the skillet and
heat over medium heat. Add the onion and mushrooms
and sauté until the onion begins to be translucent. Raise
the heat slightly. Add the chicken and bacon and cook,
uncovered, until the juices run clear when the chicken is
pierced with a fork, about 15 minutes on each side. Add
more oil as needed while the chicken cooks.

Remove the chicken from the skillet, drain on paper
towels and keep warm. Drain the excess oil from the
skillet. Scrape the skillet with a fork to loosen any bits
that stick to the skillet. Add the reserved flour and stir
until golden. Add the milk and 1/2 cup of warm water
and cook, stirring constantly, until the gravy thickens.
Season with salt and freshly ground black pepper. Pour
the gravy over the chicken and sprinkle with the paprika.
Serve immediately with rice (page 98) or mashed potatoes.

♫ PACIFIC OVERTURES ♫

Book by John Weidman
Music and lyrics by Stephen Sondheim
Opened January 11, 1976, at the Winter Garden Theatre

Preparing to direct this fact-based musical about Nippon, the Floating Kingdom, an island empire striving to protect its peaceful society from Western intrusion, Harold Prince spent ten days in Japan, watching performances of Noh and Kabuki. From among the elements of these traditional Japanese theatre forms, Prince adapted the hanamichi or "flower pathway," men playing women's roles and black-gowned stage hands who change sets as the audience watches.

The actual invasion of Japan was a risky undertaking for Commodore Perry aboard the U.S.S. *Powhatan* in 1851, and creating a musical more about ideas than about people and actions proved equally so for the authors of *Pacific Overtures*. The show closed after only 193 performances.

Tradition governed the musical and the performance. Using the reciter from Kabuki and Bunraku plays, the authors explain:

> The arrangement of rice.
> The farmer plants the rice.
> The priest exalts the rice.
> The lord collects the rice.
> The merchant buys the rice.

We invite you to take the process a few steps further -- to cooking, serving and eating the rice.

FLOATING KINGDOM RICE

For a party of 4-6.   Preparation time: about 30 minutes.

1 cup white rice
2 cups clear chicken stock
2 tablespoon canola, safflower or extra virgin olive oil
1 red onion, chopped
1 clove garlic, minced
1 red bell pepper, seeds and membranes removed,
    chopped
Zest of 1 orange, grated
Juice of 1 orange

In a large saucepan, combine the rice and stock and bring to a boil, uncovered, over high heat. Immediately reduce the heat to simmer, cover and cook for 15 minutes. Remove from the heat and allow to stand for about 5 minutes.

While the rice cooks, heat the oil in a large skillet. Add the onion and sauté until translucent. Add the garlic and bell pepper and sauté for 5 minutes. Stir in the rice, orange zest and juice and cook, stirring constantly, until most of the liquid has evaporated but the rice is still moist. Serve hot.

If you prefer your rice in a pudding, a recipe appears on page 144.   A recipe for pilaf appears on page 125.

And if you'd like to boil your rice in the Oriental tradition, follow the instructions in the first paragraph above, substituting 2 cups of water for the stock and not adding any other ingredients to the rice.

♫ THE BEST LITTLE ♫
WHOREHOUSE IN TEXAS

Book by Larry L. King and Peter Masterson
Music and lyrics by Carol Hall
Opened April 17, 1978, at the Entermedia Theatre

Larry King started it all with an article in *Playboy* magazine about a brothel in a small Texas town that had been subsidized by local bureaucrats for the past hundred years. Masterson, an actor, read the article and convinced fellow Texans King and Hall to create a musical. With this amiable view of small town activities and a romanticized approach toward the whorehouse and the effects of unemployment upon its workers, the writers caricatured the do-gooders in chronicling the fall of an institution. Tommy Tune's choreography added to the entertainment with such sequences as the "locker room dance." After moving from Off-Broadway to the Forty-Sixth Street Theatre in June of 1978, the musical was chosen as a "Best Play" and became the first country-western musical to make a profit on Broadway.

Early in Act I, Scene 1, audiences learn that the "Best Little Whorehouse in Texas" is known as a Chicken Ranch -- "the girls began accepting poultry in trade."

The Farmer pulls a chicken out of the bag and holds it out proudly to barter.

THE BEST LITTLE CHICKEN IN TEXAS

For a party of 4-6. Preparation time: about 50 minutes.

1 small onion, finely minced
1-2 cloves garlic, finely minced
3/4 cup catsup

2 teaspoons Worcestershire sauce
2 tablespoons Dijon mustard
1/4 cup light brown sugar
2 tablespoons vinegar
1/4 teaspoon crushed red pepper
1 fryer, cut into serving pieces (skin may be removed for a
    lower fat dish)
Salt and freshly ground black pepper, to taste

In a small bowl, mix together the onion, garlic, catsup, Worcestershire sauce, mustard, brown sugar, vinegar and red pepper. Season the chicken with salt and pepper, to taste. Coat the chicken lightly with part of the sauce mixture and let stand for 30 minutes. Reserve the remaining sauce.

Preheat the broiler. Broil the chicken, beginning with the skin side down, for 20 minutes on each side, basting every 10 minutes with the reserved sauce. Serve immediately.

♬

In Act II, Scene 2, Mona tells of a night in Galveston (with the Sheriff!):

> We had a champagne brunch and I ordered Eggs Benedict, which I thought sounded mighty high-toned. I didn't even realize the chef had messed up the hollandaise sauce.

MONA'S EGGS BENEDICT

For a party of 6. Preparation time: about 30 minutes.

6 large eggs
6 slices ham
3 English muffins (we like whole wheat muffins for this
    dish)
1 1/2 cups Hollandaise sauce (page 182)

The day before serving, but not more than 24 hours in advance, poach the eggs: Place 1 1/2" of water in a large skillet and bring to a full, rolling boil. When the water is boiling, reduce the heat. When the water stills, break the eggs, one at a time, into a cup. Tilt the cup until the edge is even with the surface of the water and allow the egg to slide gently into the water. Simmer each egg for 3-5 minutes, or until the white is firm and the yolk appears to be pink. Using a slotted spoon, remove the eggs from the water and drain well. Trim off and discard any "streamers" that have formed on the whites. Place the eggs in a bowl of ice water and refrigerate until ready to serve.

Remove the eggs from the ice water and drain well. Heat the ham, toast the muffins and keep both warm. Prepare the Hollandaise sauce. Place a slice of ham on each muffin. Top each with an egg. Smother immediately with the sauce and serve immediately -- with champagne!

♫ **SWEENEY TODD** ♫
THE DEMON BARBER OF FLEET STREET

Book by Hugh Wheeler
Music and lyrics by Stephen Sondheim
Opened March 1, 1979, at the Uris Theatre

An adaptation of a Victorian thriller in which melodramatic madness is juxtaposed with demonic comedy, *Sweeney Todd* became a metaphor of dehumanization for producer Harold Prince. To create the appropriate setting for his vision of symbolically and theatrically "separating people from the sun," Prince purchased a derelict factory in Rhode Island, transported it to Manhattan and reconstructed it on the stage of the Uris Theatre. His efforts paid off: *Sweeney Todd* won a Tony Award for Best Musical, the New York Drama Critics' Circle Award and the Outer Critics' Circle Award. Len Cariou was cast as the demented barber who slices up his customers in his quest for revenge, and Angela Lansbury played Mrs. Lovett, who conveniently cooks up meat pies of suspicious origin. In spite of a run of 558 performances in New York and a successful national tour, the musical was, ironically, a failure in London.

Mrs. Lovett and her pie shop are first seen early in Act I. Sweeney Todd is her first customer for weeks. Business is down because, as she admits, her pies are "only lard and nothing more." By Act II, things -- including her recipe -- have changed. Mrs. Lovett now has a "modest outdoor eating garden" where customers relish her pies and guzzle ale. Her secret, she confides, is a "family secret, all to do with herbs." Later, she elaborates on her pie-making process:

And you know the secret that makes the pies so sweet and tender? Three times. You must put the meat through the grinder three times.

And that isn't Mrs. Lovett's only secret. Needless to say, we don't follow her recipe to the letter, and -- for the sake of happy endings -- we strongly suggest that you do not, either.

MRS. LOVETT'S MEAT PIES (WITH VARIATIONS*)

For a party of 6.   Preparation time: about 3 hours.

For the filling:
1 tablespoon margarine
1 tablespoon flour
1 cup beef stock
1 pound high quality ground *beef, pork or lamb (or any combination of these)
1 large potato, grated
1 medium onion, finely chopped
1/8 teaspoon salt
1/4 teaspoon freshly ground black pepper
1/2 teaspoon dried basil
1/4 teaspoon dried oregano
1 tablespoon (or more) chopped fresh cilantro leaves

For the crust:
2 cups unbleached flour
2 teaspoons vegetable shortening
1/2 teaspoon salt

Preheat the oven to 275°.   Melt the margarine in a small saucepan over medium heat. Add the flour and stir to make a paste. Add the stock slowly and cook, stirring constantly, until the liquid reaches the consistency of gravy. Set aside.

[If you really want to be true to Mrs. Lovett's process, now is the time to place the meat in a grinder and (never mind that it's already ground) grind 3 times!]

Combine the meat, potato, onion, salt, pepper, basil and oregano.

Make the crust: In a large bowl, combine the flour, shortening, salt and enough water to make a manageable dough. Divide the dough into 2 equal portions and, on a well floured surface, roll out 2 circles. Line a pie pan with one of the circles, add the filling and sprinkle with the cilantro. Top the pie with the remaining crust circle. Seal the edges of the crust with your fingers or a fork. Pierce the top crust several times with the fork. Bake about 2 hours and 30 minutes. Serve immediately.

♫ SUGAR BABIES ♫

Book by Ralph G. Allen, with Harry Rigby
Music by Jimmy McHugh
Lyrics by Dorothy Fields and Al Dubin
Opened October 8, 1979, at the Mark Hellinger Theatre

This burlesque musical, chosen "Best Play" by critics, was brought to life by the dancing and comic flair of Ann Miller and the low clowning of Mickey Rooney. Ann Jillian was also in the cast. Based on famous burlesque acts of the past -- the old gags of the comedians and the saucy routines of the strippers (such as Gypsy Rose Lee and Sally Rand) -- the sketches evoke the naughty laughter of an age gone by.

Act II, Scene 7 "Poetic Justice"
Woman: How much is a nice filet mignon?
Waiter: Sixty-two cents.
[We learn that the waiter's boss is uptown with the waiter's wife.]
What he's doing to her, I'm doing to him.

Scenes, songs and jokes maintain a rapid pace that kept *Sugar Babies* on Broadway for months.

Act I, Scene 3 "Sugar Babies"
Let me be your sugar baby
Let me be your danish pastry

DANISH PASTRIES

Makes 24 pastries. Preparation time: about 2 hours.

For the crust:
8 ounces Neufchâtel cheese, softened
2 2/3 sticks margarine, softened
2 2/3 cups unbleached flour

For the filling:
3 1/2 cups coarsely chopped walnuts
1 1/2 cups coarsely chopped dried dates
1 1/2 cups drained and coarsely chopped maraschino
    cherries

For the topping:
2 cups brown sugar
3 eggs, slightly beaten
3 tablespoons melted margarine

In a large bowl, cream together the cheese and sticks of margarine. Add the flour, a bit at a time, and blend thoroughly into a dough. Divide the dough into 24 walnut-sized balls. On a well floured surface, roll out each ball into a 4" circle. (Wrap any remaining dough in plastic wrap and refrigerate for future use.) Line each of 24 well greased 2" muffin cups with a circle of dough.

Preheat the oven to 350°. In a large bowl, mix thoroughly the walnuts, dates and cherries and place an equal amount of filling in each lined cup.

Combine the brown sugar, eggs and melted margarine and beat until the sugar is completely dissolved and the ingredients are well blended. Being careful not to spill the topping on the crust or the muffin tins, pour the mixture evenly over the pastries.

Bake the pastries for 20 minutes. Cool for about 15 minutes in the tins on wire racks. Remove from the tins and serve warm or at room temperature.

♬

Act I, Scene 5 "In Lou'siana"
    I miss the candied yams
        In Lou'siana
    Miss the shrimps and hams
        In Lou'siana

LOU'SIANA CANDIED YAMS

For a party of 6. Preparation time: about 45 minutes.

3 large sweet potatoes, peeled and cut into 1 1/2" chunks
1/4 cup stick margarine, melted
1/2 cup brown sugar
1/2 teaspoon pure vanilla extract
Zest of 2 lemons, grated

In a large saucepan bring to boil enough water to cover the potatoes. Place the potatoes in the pan and boil until tender, about 15 minutes. Drain, reserving about 2 tablespoons of the cooking liquid.

Preheat the oven to 350°. Mix together the margarine, brown sugar, vanilla extract, lemon zest and reserved cooking liquid. Place the potatoes in a baking dish that has been coated with non-stick spray, pour the margarine mixture over the potatoes and bake for about 20 minutes, basting once or twice with the baking juices. Serve immediately.

♫ **WOMAN OF THE YEAR** ♫

Book by Peter Stone   Music by John Kander
Lyrics by Fred Ebb
Opened March 29, 1981, at the Palace Theatre

Lauren Bacall as Tess Harding, TV interviewer and commentator, produced some excitement among critics with this visit to Broadway.   Much of the conflict in *Woman of the Year* depends upon Tess' contretemps with a cartoonist, played by Harry Guardino, and those friends who would run her life.   It is one of the few musicals that actually has a recipe in it.   To celebrate her husband's birthday (Act II, Scene 5), Tess will bake a cake on TV -- from a recipe by Craig Claiborne:

> Birthday Cake: Two cups flour, two teaspoons baking powder, two eggs separated, one teaspoon salt, one cup milk, one teaspoon vanilla, one cup sugar, one half cup shortening . . . Preheat oven to three-seventy-five.

Who would argue with Craig Claiborne?   But we don't wholeheartedly recommend Tess's technique, particularly when "the cake starts to ooze out of the oven"!

At a Third Avenue saloon, Tess and the cartoonist stop to eat (I, 5):

> Manny, the proprietor: The specialty tonight is corned beef and cabbage.   Jules Feiffer discovered the original Dinty Moore recipe in "Bringing Up Father" in 1926.

Ours is not the original Dinty Moore recipe, and we suspect that Manny may be pulling someone's leg.   We hope you'll find the following recipe satisfactory, none the less.

MANNY'S CORNED BEEF AND CABBAGE

For a party of 6.   Preparation time: about 3 hours and 15 minutes.

2 1/2 pounds corned beef
4 medium carrots, scraped and chopped into 1/2" - 3/4" rounds
2 medium turnips, peeled and cut into 1/2" - 3/4" cubes
6 medium potatoes, cut into 1" cubes
6 small onions, peeled
1/2 head cabbage, cut into wedges, 1" at their thickest
Salt and freshly ground black pepper, to taste

In a large pot, cover the corned beef with cold water. Bring to a boil over high heat. Immediately reduce the heat to simmer, cover and cook for about 2 hours and 30 minutes, or until the beef is tender, occasionally skimming off any foam that forms on top. Add the vegetables and simmer, uncovered, for at least 30 minutes, or until very tender. Season with salt and pepper and serve immediately.

♬

In Act II, Scene 4, Tess visits Larry, the happiest of men, and Jan, the woman who makes him so.

Jan: What can I tell you? You know everything.
Tess: Yeah, but that's <u>all</u> I know. I can't <u>do</u> anything.
    Look at you -- you can <u>do</u> everything.
(Song: "The Grass is Always Greener.")
Tess: You can make a pot roast.
    That's wonderful!
Jan: What's so wonderful
    First, you brown an onion . . .

JAN'S POT ROAST

For a party of 8.   Preparation time: about 3 hours and 45 minutes.

1 4- to 5-pound beef chuck roast
Flour
2-3 tablespoons unsalted butter or margarine
1 large onion, coarsely chopped
8-10 medium carrots, scraped and cut into 1" rounds
8-10 celery stalks, cut into 1" slices
8 small new potatoes in their jackets
Salt and freshly ground black pepper, to taste

Roll the roast in the flour and set aside. Melt the butter in a large pot over medium heat, add the onion and sauté for about 5 minutes. Add the roast and brown on all sides, adding more butter if necessary. Add about 1 cup of cold water, bring to a boil, reduce the heat to simmer, cover and cook for 3 hours, or until the meat is tender. Add the vegetables and simmer, uncovered, for about 30 minutes, or until the potatoes are tender. Season with salt and pepper and serve hot.

♫ NINE ♫

Book by Arthur Kopit   Music and lyrics by Maury Veston
Opened May 9, 1982, at the Forty-Sixth Street Theatre

Based on Federico Fellini's autobiographical *8 1/2*, *Nine* explores the problems of a struggling filmmaker, Guido Contini, played by Raul Julia. Having had three flops in a row, Guido is trying desperately to get an idea for a film, while being haunted by numerous women -- both real and fantasized -- from the nuns of his childhood, who taught him about women, to his latest conquest. *Nine* was the first effort at musical comedy for playwright Kopit, whose *Oh Dad, Poor Dad, Mama's Hung You in the Closet and I'm Feelin' So Sad* launched his career in 1960.

Pampered and temperamental, Guido is convinced that a visit to Fontane di Luna, a health spa in Venice, will revive his creative impulses. Among the most welcome patrons at the spa are the wealthy and demanding Germans whose approach panics the chambermaids:

> I'll cool the beer
> I'll shell the prawns.
>> They're here.

To please everyone at your spa (or your dinner table), we suggest the following recipe:

PRAWNS FONTANE DI LUNA

For a party of 6.   Preparation time: about 30 minutes.

1 1/2 cups white rice
1 tablespoon olive oil
1 tablespoon unsalted butter or margarine
1 large red onion, finely chopped
1 clove garlic, finely minced
1/2 teaspoon dried oregano
1 teaspoon dried basil

2 ripe tomatoes, peeled, seeded and coarsely chopped
2 cups shelled prawns
Freshly grated Parmesan cheese
Fresh basil, for garnish

In a large saucepan, combine the rice with 3 cups of water and bring to a boil, uncovered, over high heat. Immediately reduce the heat to simmer, cover and cook for 15 minutes. Remove from the heat. Let stand for 5 minutes.

While the rice cooks, heat the oil and butter in a large skillet over medium heat. Add the onion and sauté until just tender. Add the garlic, oregano and basil and sauté for 2 minutes. Add the tomatoes and cook, stirring frequently, for 5 minutes. Add the prawns and cook just until evenly pink. Do not overcook!

Spoon the prawns and their sauce over the rice, top with the cheese and garnish with the basil. Serve immediately.

♫

A little later in Act I, Guido remembers his childhood in song in "The Bells of St. Sebastian."

For lunch at St. Sebastian Country
Cheese and buttered bread.

For all its bland appearance, this luncheon dish is a treat!

ST. SEBASTIAN CHEESE AND BUTTERED BREAD

2 loaves Italian bread, cut into 1/2" slices
1 stick unsalted butter or margarine, softened
8 ounces Saga Bleu cheese

Preheat the oven to 375°. Spread each slice of bread with butter and cheese. Place in a single layer on ungreased cookie sheets and bake for about 7 minutes. Serve warm.

♫ CATS ♫

Based on *Old Possum's Book of Practical Cats* by T. S. Eliot
Music by Andrew Lloyd Webber
Opened in America October 7, 1982,
at the Winter Garden Theatre

Few students of American/English literature fully appreciate T. S. Eliot's light and frivolous view of life as revealed in *Old Possum's Book of Practical Cats.* Many think of Eliot only as the creator of J. Alfred Prufrock, or as a serious poet concerned with the decay of Western culture in *The Waste Land* or the relationship between time and eternity which he explained in *The Four Quartets.* For the theatre, he wrote a number of plays -- *Murder in the Cathedral*, 1935, his best known -- which had an enormous influence upon intellectuals. When he received the Nobel Prize for Literature in 1948, it was his reputation in the modern Symbolist-metaphysical tradition that was celebrated. It took the inspiration of Andrew Lloyd Webber to bring Eliot's "common touch" to the attention of the vast musical theatre audience.

The *Book of Practical Cats* is a series of comically descriptive commentaries on a number of fascinating felines, all immediately recognizable to cat fanciers. There is, for example, the Rum Tum Tugger, artful and knowing:

> If you offer him pheasant, he would rather have
> grouse.
> The Rum Tum Tugger is a curious beast.
> If you offer him fish then he always wants a feast;
> Where there isn't any fish then he won't eat rabbit
> His disobliging ways are a matter of habbit.

THE RUM TUM TUGGER'S REJECTED RABBITS

For a party of 6-8.   Preparation time: about 1 hour.

2 fresh rabbits, cleaned and cut into serving pieces
4 tablespoons flour
3-4 tablespoons canola or safflour oil
Juice of 3 oranges
Zest of 3 oranges, grated
1/8 teaspoon (or less) salt
1 1/2 tablespoons cornstarch
1/4 cup sugar
1/4 cup finely chopped green bell pepper
1/4 cup finely chopped red bell pepper
2 oranges, unpeeled, cut into chunks with seeds removed

Dredge the rabbit pieces in the flour to coat evenly on all sides. Heat the oil in a very large skillet, or two smaller skillets, over medium heat. Add the rabbit and cook to brown evenly on all sides. Add the orange juice, zest and salt, reduce the heat to simmer, cover and cook until the rabbit is tender, about 40 minutes. Remove the meat to a warm platter, reserving the liquid in the skillet. In a bowl, combine the cornstarch and sugar with 1/2 cup of water. Pour into the reserved liquid, stirring to blend. Add the bell pepper and orange chunks and simmer for 5 minutes, stirring constantly. Pour the sauce over the meat and serve immediately.

And, of course, there's Bustopher Jones, who "is not skin and bones --"

In fact, he's remarkably fat.
If he looks full of gloom then he's lunched at the Tomb
On cabbage, rice pudding and mutton.

BUSTOPHER JONES' MUTTON

For a party of 6.   Preparation time: about 1 hour.

2 tablespoons flour
1/8 teaspoon (or less) salt
1/2 teaspoon freshly ground black pepper
6 lamb shoulder chops
1 tablespoon extra virgin olive oil
1 small red onion, peeled and diced
1/4 cup catsup
1 bay leaf
1 cup cooked peas

Mix together the flour, salt and pepper. Dredge the lamb chops in the flour to coat evenly. Heat the oil in a large skillet over medium-high heat. Add the chops and sear until brown on one side. Add the onion, turn the chops and sear until brown on the other side. Add the catsup, the bay leaf and enough water to cover the chops. Reduce the heat to simmer and cook until the lamb is tender, about 45 minutes. Add the peas and simmer to heat through. Serve immediately with rice (see page 98) and cabbage.

If your remarkable cats prefer lamb shish kebabs, see the recipe on page 125. And another recipe for lamb chops appears on page 185.

BUSTOPHER'S CABBAGE

For a party of 6.   Preparation time: about 20 minutes.

5 cups shredded fresh cabbage
Salt and freshly ground black pepper, to taste
2 tablespoons unsalted butter or margarine
2 tablespoons flour
1 cup milk

Bring enough cold water to cover the cabbage to a boil in a large saucepan. Add the cabbage, reduce the heat so that the water maintains the boil but does not boil over. Cook for about 10 minutes. Drain the cabbage and sprinkle with the salt and pepper. Melt the butter in the saucepan over medium-low heat. Stir in the flour. Add the milk, a bit at a time, stirring constantly to dissolve any lumps. Add the cabbage and toss gently. Reduce the heat to low and cook for 5 minutes, stirring frequently. Serve immediately.

For Bustopher's Rice Pudding, see the recipe on page 144.

♬ # SUNDAY IN THE PARK ♬
WITH GEORGE

Book by James Lapine
Music and lyrics by Stephen Sondheim
Opened May 2, 1984, at the Booth Theatre

Inspired by Georges Seurat's great painting, *A Sunday Afternoon on the Island of La Grande Jatte*, this wholly original musical marked the first collaborative work of the authors. Setting the first act in the 1880's, when the painting was created, and the second act a hundred years later, among descendants of Seurat and his model, Sondheim and Lapine explored the artist's struggle. One critic noted that Act I dramatizes the making of art, Act II the making of life. An ambitious undertaking, *Sunday in the Park with George* won the Pulitzer Prize for drama and the Drama Critics' Circle Award for Best Musical. Mandy Patinkin played both the painter and his descendant, and Bernadette Peters played Dot and Marie.

In the title song in Act I Dot, Seurat's model, voices a complaint.

> Well, if you want bread
> And respect
> And attention
> Not to say connection
> Modeling's no profession.

From this point on, bread is used as a sexual metaphor and recurring motif. As George sketches a boatman from an island in the Seine, Dot appears arm-in-arm with Louis the baker. Two shop girls giggle, and one says: "She knows how to make dough rise!" Dot sings:

> The bread, George,
> I mean the bread, George

And men in bed, George . . .
I mean he kneads me --
I mean like dough, George . . .
Hello, George . . .
[But Louis is the subject of her song.]
    Louis's really an artist:
    Louis's cakes are an art.
    Everybody loves Louis.
    Louis bakes from the heart.

And strolling on the island, an American Southern couple find that they do not much care for the French, but they adore the baker's art, as we think you will, too.

FRENCH BREAD BAKED FROM THE HEART

Makes 2 loaves.   Preparation time: about 4 hours and 30 minutes, including rising and baking.

1/2 cup milk
1 cake compressed yeast
1 1/2 cups melted shortening
5 teaspoons sugar
4 cups sifted all-purpose flour
1 teaspoon salt

For the glaze:
1 egg white

Scald the milk (do not boil!) and add 1 cup of boiling water.   Allow to cool to 85°.   Meanwhile, dissolve the yeast in 1/4 cup of 85° water.   Allow the yeast to rest for 10 minutes, then add to the milk mixture, along with the shortening and 1 tablespoon of the sugar.

In another bowl combine the flour, salt and remaining sugar.   Make a hole in the center of this mixture and pour in the milk mixture.   Stir to blend thoroughly (do not knead!).   Cover the dough with a clean, damp cloth and allow to rise in a warm place for about 2 hours. Using your fist, punch down the dough. On a well floured board, pat the dough into two equal oblongs. Using your hands, shape the dough into loaves by rolling each oblong away from you, pressing outward and tapering the ends until each loaf is long and thin. Place the loaves on a greased baking sheet and make diagonal slits 1/4" deep across the top of each loaf. Allow to rise until approximately doubled in size.

Meanwhile, preheat the oven to 400°. Place a pan filled with 1/2" boiling water on the bottom of the oven. Bake the bread for 15 minutes, reduce the heat to 350° and bake for about 25 minutes longer. Beat the egg white, mix with the 1 tablespoon of cold water and brush each loaf. Bake for about 5 minutes.

♫ NUNSENSE ♫

Book, music and lyrics by Dan Goggin
Opened December 12, 1985, at the Cherry Lane Theatre

Founded in Seventh Century England by Saint Wilfred, the Order of the Little Sisters of Hoboken finally came to America. In this playful commentary on the activities of the Order, food is of major importance. In Act II, Sister Amnesia explains that in order to earn money for a particular purpose, the Sisters are planning to publish a cookbook: *Baking with the B.V.M.* (Blessed Virgin Mary), by Sister Julia. "Full of unusual recipes: Cesar Franck's Panis Angelicus -- a delightful taste treat consisting of two hot dogs, wrapped in anchovies, and served on a slice of Wonder bread."

This is the same Sister Julia who started the difficulty in the first place, as the Reverend Mother reports in the opening scene:

> Reverend Mother: You see, a short time ago, our cook, Sister Julia -- Child of God, served some vichyssoise soup and nearly every sister died instantly of botulism.
> Sister Mary Hubert: It was kind of like the "Last Supper." (pause) That's a little convent humor.

It seems that all the unfortunate sisters were buried, except for four, who are being kept in the freezer until enough money is earned for their burial. Hence, the sale of the cookbook!

It is not our purpose to compete with the B.V.M., in matters culinary or otherwise, but may we suggest a safer version of vichyssoise?

VICHYSSOISE

For a party of 6.   Preparation time: 1 hour, plus chilling.

4 large potatoes, peeled and sliced
4 large leeks, white and about 2" of green parts, split
    lengthwise, washed thoroughly and thinly sliced
2 stalks celery, cut into 2" pieces
1 white onion, sliced
5 cups clear chicken stock
1/2 teaspoon (or less) salt
1 cup milk
1/2 teaspoon freshly ground white pepper
1 cup heavy cream
Chopped fresh chive, for garnish

Place the potatoes, leeks, celery, onion and chicken stock in a large saucepan. Bring to a boil, immediately reduce the heat to simmer, partially cover and cook for 45 minutes, or until the vegetables are tender. Remove from the heat and add 1/4 teaspoon salt. Puree the mixture in a blender, or work through a food mill. Return the mixture to the saucepan, add the milk and bring to a simmer over low heat. Cook for 5 minutes. Pass the mixture through a fine sieve. Add the pepper and more salt, if needed. Blend in the cream. Chill the soup until very cold before serving in chilled bowls. Garnish with the fresh chive.

♬

In Act II Sister Leo reports that Sister Julia -- Child of God -- "was trying out a new Chinese Dish -- Chicken with Sudafeds -- or something like that -- anyway, it backfired and she's in the hospital getting her stomach pumped."

For chicken recipes that (although they are not Chinese and contain no Sudafeds) will not backfire, see pages 6, 37, 105, 128, 154 and 158.

♫ INTO THE WOODS ♫

Book by James Lapine
Music and lyrics by Stephen Sondheim
Opened November 5, 1987, at the Martin Beck Theatre

"In a far-off Kingdom . . . lived a young maiden . . . a sad lad . . . and a childless baker . . . with his wife." With this situation for starters and, with the assistance of Cinderella, Jack (of Beanstalk fame), Little Red Riding Hood, Rapunzel and the persistent Baker, the authors suggest serious consequences:

Into the woods, each time you go,
There's more to learn of what you know.

Bernadette Peters excited audiences as the Witch, and Joanna Gleason received a Tony Award for her performance as the Baker's Wife. As the character who stimulates much of the action, the Witch, as revealed by her garden, exhibits a very limited view of food:

Greens, greens, and nothing but greens;
Parsley, peppers, cabbage and celery,
Asparagus and watercress and
Fiddleferns and lettuce --!
[She is particularly possessive of her "special beans."]
Don't ever never ever
Mess around with my greens!
Especially the beans.

Keeping her warning in mind, we will pass by the beans with this simple suggestion: Snip the ends off twice as many handfuls of fresh young green beans as there are members of your party, wash the beans under cold running water, place them over boiling water in a steamer pan and steam until bright green and just tender. And turn the page for ideas for some of the Witch's other greens.

181

FIDDLEFERNS

For a party of 6.   Preparation time: about 30 minutes.

6 bunches, about 8 fronds each, of ostrich fern
    fiddleheads*, washed and tied with string

For the Hollandaise sauce:
1/2 cup butter
1 1/2 tablespoons tarragon vinegar or fresh lemon juice
    (not bottled juice!)
3 egg yolks
1/8 teaspoon (or less) salt
A pinch of cayenne pepper

In a tall pot, bring 1/2 cup of water to a boil. Stand the
bunches of ferns upright in the water, cover tightly,
reduce the heat to simmer and cook for 20 minutes, or
until tender.

While the ferns cook, make the Hollandaise sauce: Melt
the butter over very low heat and keep warm. Heat the
vinegar until just warm. Place the egg yolks in the top of
a double boiler over, not in, simmering water. Beat the
yolks with a wire whisk until they begin to thicken. Add,
1 at a time, 4 tablespoons of hot water, beating after each
addition until the egg yolks begin to thicken again. Beat
in the vinegar. Remove the boiler from the heat and
continue to beat the sauce with the wire whisk. Beating
constantly, drizzle in the melted butter and add the salt
and cayenne pepper. As soon as the sauce is thick, pour it
over the fiddleheads and serve immediately.

*Fiddlehead ferns grow wild in shaded, wooded areas.
Harvest them in the springtime, while the shoots are still
tightly curled.

ASPARAGUS SOUP

For a party of 6.   Preparation time: about 35 minutes.

2 pounds thin stalks fresh asparagus, scales removed
5 cups clear chicken stock
1/4 teaspoon Kosher salt
1 large onion, peeled
2 stalks celery, cut into 2"- 3" pieces
5-6 sprigs fresh parsley or Italian parsley
1 tablespoon cornstarch
4 tablespoons unsalted butter or margarine, softened
1/2 cup heavy cream or half-and-half
Salt and freshly ground white pepper, to taste
Paprika

Cut the tips from the asparagus and set aside. Cut the
stalks diagonally into 3/4" slices. In a large saucepan,
combine the stock and Kosher salt and bring to a boil.
Add the asparagus slices, onion, celery and parsley, reduce
the heat to simmer and cook for about 15 minutes. Add
the asparagus tips and simmer for 5 minutes more. Using
a slotted spoon, remove the vegetables from the pan,
discarding the onion, celery and parsley. Keep the stock
simmering. Mix the cornstarch with 2 tablespoons of cold
water and stir into the stock. Raise the heat and, stirring
constantly, return the stock to a boil. Immediately lower
the heat and stir in the butter and cream. Return the
asparagus to the pan and cook for about 4 minutes longer.
Season with salt and white pepper. Sprinkle with paprika
and serve immediately.

For recipes for cabbage, see pages 168 and 174.

♫ THE PHANTOM ♫ OF THE OPERA

Book by Andrew Lloyd Webber, with Richard Stilgoe
Music by Andrew Lloyd Webber
Lyrics by Charles Hart, with Richard Stilgoe
Opened October 9, 1986, in London,
January 26, 1988, at the Majestic Theatre

History tells us that M. Gaston Leroux's 1911 novel attracted little attention, and film versions of *The Phantom of the Opera* with Lon Chaney (1925), Claude Rains (1943) and Herbert Lom (1962) built upon the reputations of the actors. Webber's adaptation of this show-must-go-on piece depends substantially upon the premiere production by Harold Prince and the performances of Sarah Brightman (Mrs. Webber) as Christine and Michael Crawford as the Phantom. The story is quickly and boldly told through Webber's soaring melodies which, as outpourings from the heart of the Phantom (who is also known as the Angel of Music), must enchant the audience as well as Christine.

In Act II, Scene 7, as the Phantom prepares to play the final scene of "Don Juan Triumphant" with Christine as Aminta, the chorus sings:

Here the sire may serve the dam,
   here the master takes his meat!
Here the sacrifical lamb
   utters one despairing bleat!
Chorus and Carlotta: Serve the meal and serve the
   maid!
   leave the master so that, when
   tables, plans and maids are laid,
   Don Juan triumphs once again!

DON JUAN'S SACRIFICIAL LAMB CHOPS

For a party of 6.   Preparation time: about 45 minutes.

3-4 Irish potatoes, peeled and cut into 1" chunks
3 tablespoons milk
1 tablespoon unsalted butter
Salt and freshly ground black pepper, to taste
1 teaspoon dried thyme
6 strips bacon
6 lamb loin chops, 1 1/2" thick, bones removed
18 Brussels sprouts
3 cups mashed potatoes
Sprigs of fresh thyme or lemon thyme, for garnish

Bring enough water to cover the potatoes to a boil in a large saucepan. Add the potatoes and cook, uncovered, for about 15 minutes, or until tender. Drain, return to the pan, add the milk and butter and mash until smooth. Season with salt and pepper. Keep warm.

Preheat the broiler.   Season each chop with salt, pepper and dried thyme. Roll each chop and then roll a strip of bacon around each chop, securing with small skewers. Brown the chops 3" below the broiler element, for about 7 minutes on each side, or until the bacon is well cooked.

While the chops broil, cook the Brussels sprouts over boiling water in a steamer pan until tender and bright green. Drain and keep warm.

Place each chop on an individual plank or oven-proof plate and surround with Brussels sprouts and a border of mashed potatoes pressed through a pastry tube. Place the planks under the broiler until the potatoes are browned. Serve immediately, garnished with the fresh thyme.

For other lamb recipes, see pages 125 and 174.

♫ GRAND HOTEL ♫

Book by Luther Davis
Music and lyrics by Robert Wright and George Forrest
Opened November 12, 1989, at the Martin Beck Theatre

Grand Hotel illustrates a trend of the Broadway musical away from ideas and concepts, to take advantage of vintage Hollywood films. In this instance Vicki Baum's novel, set in the Grand Hotel in Berlin, "the world's most expensive hotel," in 1928, came to New York via California. With John Wylie as Colonel Doctor Ottemschlay, the musical won five Tony Awards.

The Coffee Bar in Scene 2 is probably not the kind of place where one might expect to dine well. In Scene 4, however, the Baron, having followed his prey into the Ladies' Cloakroom, attempts to ingratiate himself with the question: "Did I hear you say you like caviar?" The Baron does not receive a response, but we would suggest that in the Grand Hotel dining room you could most certainly find caviar, as well as some other delicacies.

PATÉ MAISON GRAND HOTEL

For a party of 12. Preparation time: about 3 hours, plus chilling.

1/4 cup whipping cream
4 slices bacon, chopped
1 cup thinly sliced salt pork
1 1/2 pounds chicken livers
3 eggs
3 tablespoons brandy
2 tablespoons port wine
1/4 cup flour
2 teaspoons finely ground fresh ginger root

1 teaspoon salt
1 teaspoon freshly ground black pepper
1 teaspoon allspice
1-2 minced truffles

Whip the cream and set aside. Preheat the oven to 325°. Blanch and drain the bacon and the salt pork, keeping them separate. Divide the chicken livers into 3 equal portions. In a blender, mix the first portion with the bacon, 1 egg, the brandy, port wine and flour. Blend the second portion with the remaining 2 eggs. Gently fold the whipped cream into the third portion. Gently combine the 3 portions and mix lightly with the ginger root, salt, pepper, allspice and truffles. Place the mixture in a greased loaf pan and top with the salt pork. Insert a meet thermometer. Cover the pan as tightly as possible with heavy-duty foil. Place the loaf pan in a larger pan and fill the larger pan with boiling water to reach halfway up the side of the loaf pan. Carefully place both pans in the oven and bake for about 2 hours, or until your meat thermometer reaches 180°. Allow the paté to cool enough to refrigerate.

Chill the paté, remove any excess fat from the surface, and serve cold with sliced French bread and baby pickles.

CHEF'S SPECIAL CHOCOLATE CAKE

For a party of 10-12. Preparation time: about 1 hour, plus cooling.

For the cake:
4 squares unsweetened chocolate
4 tablespoons unsalted butter or margarine
2 cups sifted all-purpose flour
1/2 teaspoon salt
2 cups sugar
1 egg
1 3/4 cups milk

1 teaspoon pure vanilla extract
1 teaspoon baking soda

For the frosting:
3/4 cup sugar
1/4 cup bakers cocoa
2 tablespoons cornstarch
1 cup milk
1 tablespoon unsalted butter
1 teaspoon pure vanilla extract

Preheat the oven to 350°. In a saucepan, melt the chocolate and butter. Pour the mixture into a mixing bowl and allow to cool slightly. In another bowl sift together the flour and salt and set aside. Add the sugar to the chocolate and blend thoroughly. Add the egg and 1 cup of the milk to the chocolate mixture and stir to blend. Sift the flour mixture into the chocolate mixture and beat until the flour is well moistened. Continue beating by hand for 1 minute. Add the vanilla extract and 1/2 cup of the remaining milk and beat to blend thoroughly. Dissolve the baking soda in the remaining milk and quickly mix into the cake batter. Pour the batter into 2 well greased and floured 8" or 9" pans and bake for 35-40 minutes, or until a toothpick inserted in the center of the cake comes out clean. Cool on racks for a few minutes before removing from the pans. Cool completely before frosting.

While the cake cools, make the frosting: In a saucepan, combine the sugar, cocoa, cornstarch and milk. Cook over low to medium heat, stirring constantly, until the mixture thickens. Stir in the butter and vanilla extract and stir until the mixture reaches spreading consistency. Allow to cool completely before frosting the cake.

♫ CITY OF ANGELS ♫

Book by Larry Gelbart   Music by Cy Coleman
Lyrics by David Zippel
Opened December 11, 1989, at the Virginia Theatre

Something of a *tour de force*, *City of Angels* won several awards -- the Tony, the Drama Desk, the Outer Critics Circle -- while running for 912 performances. The musical takes place in Los Angeles in the late 1940's and follows the problems of a movie scriptwriter named Stine (played by Gregg Edelman), as he plans a murder mystery based on the "Kingsley case." Interjecting his own experiences and acquaintances into the scenes and characters he is creating, Stine uses a private detective named Stone (played by James Naughton) as his alter-ego. Although *City of Angels* produced no lasting musical numbers, it effectively evokes the spirit of its time and place.

As you might expect, Stone, while pursuing the femme fatale, is arrested and threatened by the police (Act I, Scene 21), who make jokes about the most popular "last meals" served on death row. To which Stone replies:

Try a final meal of tacos on a
Plate of beans, mañana,
Odds are they are gonna
Give you gas.

Right. But please consider these recipes anyway.

DEATH ROW TACOS

For a party of 4-6. Preparation time: about 1 hour.

Note: Unlike the popular supermarket version, these tacos have soft shells!

6 ounces chorizo sausage (about 2 sausages), casings
     removed, coarsely crumbled
1 pound extra lean ground beef, coarsely crumbled

1 large onion, minced
1-2 large cloves garlic, minced
1/4 cup pitted ripe olives
8 ounces tomato sauce
1 teaspoon ground cumin
12 corn tortillas
2-3 cups shredded lettuce
1-2 tomatoes, finely chopped
2 cups shredded Monterey jack cheese
Green chili salsa
Sprigs of fresh cilantro, for garnish

Place the sausage in a large skillet and cook over medium heat, stirring frequently, for about 5 minutes. Add the ground beef a bit at a time, stirring until browned. Remove and discard any excess fat. Add the onion and garlic and cook until the onion is tender. Add the olives, tomato sauce and cumin. Bring the mixture to a boil, immediately reduce the heat to simmer, cover and cook for about 30 minutes. Remove the cover and cook, stirring frequently, until the liquid is reduced and the mixture has thickened.

Heat the tortillas according to package directions. Spoon a portion of the meat mixture onto each tortilla, top with lettuce, tomato, jack cheese and salsa. Fold each tortilla over the fillings. Garnish with fresh cilantro and serve immediately with Frijoles Refritas.

FRIJOLES REFRITAS (REFRIED BEANS)

2 tablespoons extra virgin olive oil
1 medium onion, finely chopped
1-2 cloves garlic, finely minced
1 15 1/2-ounce can light red kidney beans, drained and
    rinsed, or about 2 cups precooked dried beans
1 teaspoon ground cumin
Shredded cheddar cheese, for topping
Non-fat sour cream, for topping

In a large skillet, heat 1 tablespoon of the oil over medium heat. Add the onion and sauté until translucent. Add the garlic and sauté for about 3 minutes longer. Add the beans, cumin and 1/2 cup of water and immediately mash the beans with a fork to form a paste. If the paste becomes too thick, add more water and mash to blend thoroughly. (The onions and garlic will disappear into the paste.) Remove the paste from the skillet and set aside.

Add the second tablespoon of oil to the skillet, scraping to incorporate any bits of paste that stick to the skillet. Heat the oil over medium heat. Return the beans to the skillet and cook, stirring constantly, until heated through. If the paste becomes too thick at this point, add more water until the desired consistency is reached. Top with cheese and sour cream and serve hot, with Tacos.

Notes:

Index to Recipes

Appomattox Applesauce 115
Creamed Turnips 120
"French Fried" Parsnips 121
Claude's Mushrooms 122
Your Very Own Pilaf 125
Floating Kingdom Rice 157
Lou'siana Candied Yams 166
Bustopher's Cabbage 174
Fiddleferns 182
Frijoles Refritas 190